# 13 MOON S[illegible]

## BLUE LUNAR STORM year

July 26 2020 - July 25 2021

www.timewaves.org www.lawoftime.org

Front Cover Painting - 'STIRRINGS'
by Talitha Walterfang FB: @TalithaWalterfangArt

Back Cover Photograph 'RAINBOW NSW, AUSTRALIA 1996'
by Jethro Tanner www.jethrotanner.com

# PRAYER OF THE 7 GALACTIC DIRECTIONS

**FROM THE EAST HOUSE OF LIGHT**
May wisdom dawn in us
So we may see all things in clarity

**FROM THE SOUTH HOUSE OF NIGHT**
May wisdom ripen in us
So we may see all from within

**FROM THE WEST HOUSE OF TRANSFORMATION**
May wisdom be transformed into right action
So we may do what must be done

**FROM THE NORTH HOUSE OF THE ETERNAL SUN**
May right action reap the harvest
So we may enjoy the fruits of planetary being

**FROM ABOVE HOUSE OF HEAVEN**
Where star people and ancestors gather
May their blessings come to us now

**FROM BELOW HOUSE OF EARTH**
May the heartbeat of her crystal core
Bless us with harmony and peace to end all war

**AND FROM THE CENTRE GALACTIC SOURCE**
Which is everywhere at once
May everything be known
As the light of mutual love

**O YUM HUNAB KU EVA MAYA E MA HO!** }x3

# BLUE LUNAR STORM YEAR

Welcome to the BLUE LUNAR STORM Year. The 2nd of a 13-Year cycle. This year will act to anchor the Divine Feminine.

I Polarise in order to Catalyse
Stabilising Energy
I seal the Matrix of Self-Generation
With the Lunar Tone of Challenge
I am guided by the power of Magic

The times we are in are deeply transformative, with climate change and pandemics asking us to question the very fabric of our reality. This year asks us to reflect more deeply - What is really necessary? What is really needed? The collective shake-up will continue, questioning 'progress at all costs'?

We are learning to trust change, as the catalyst to choosing more intelligent green alternatives. We continue to educate ourselves, embracing the capacity to transform and heal our own physical cells. A shift to local markets is happening, as we question the use of export resources. Responsibility for keeping our water clean is finally more important, as we reclaim water for local use. We are facing challenges as we reclaim our world from corporate greed, while losses faced from climate change are sobering for all of us, it is the catalyst for those in power to finally change, and the Earth knows this.

We are experiencing the silver lining, as corporate greed lessens in the face of survival, intelligent conversation is beginning to be listened to, with answers which have been available for so long, qualifying the need to work together, as trust in the alternatives strengthens. It will not be an easy time, yet a lot will be learnt as the world finally begins to take seriously the change from destructive to co-creative.

For those tracking the Mayan Dreamspell codes, the daily guidance is supportive. We are on the next rung of this feminine cycle, experienced from 1967-1979, that era as the bedrock upon which this era, 2019-2031, stands. Change will occur. The sleeping masses will heed the wake-up call, for the sake of survival. The challenge to ground the new will be heard. There is reason for hope.

Vasumi, Kin 71, Blue Rhythmic Monkey

# BLUE LUNAR STORM GALACTIC VIEW BY STEPHANIE SOUTH/RQ

Blue Lunar Storm year enters us into the New Sirius Cycle 33 (1.33). This is a momentous year of world-changing proportions as we catalyse planetary energies with the opportunity for self-generation. Our task is to recognize the truth hidden behind external events.

Coded by the Lunar tone of Challenge, the Blue Lunar Storm is in the second position of the Mirror Wavespell of Endlessness. This signifies a time of self-reflection to catalyse obstacles and polarities. This year, it may feel many lifetimes are condensed into one day.

With the 7-year cycle of the New Solar Human and Sirian surveillance complete (2013-2020), we now enter the 13-year cycle to establish the Noocracy of Timeship Earth. In this 13-year cycle, we transfer the Sirian energetics to the Earth Wizards, grounding the star knowledge into the earthly realm.

Our body is an alchemical transmutation chamber, a time ship that connects to timeship earth. In this almanac, you will find the codes and keys to unearth a new consciousness. These codes of synchronicity equip us with a tool to map the patterns behind external events. These are memory codes that further activate our healing capacity by entering us into the Natural Time of the synchronic order.

The key mission of this 13-year cycle is to stabilize and unify the planetary telepathic network. But first, we must each learn to embody a new way of being that is radiating from the self-generative inner core. To reach our core requires coming fully into the Present Moment. Here, we release the grip of compulsion and obligation that suffocates our imaginal and intuitive capacities. This 13-year cycle concludes in the Blue Magnetic Storm year (2032-33).

Storm corresponds to solar/prophetic Pluto. It is the archetype of the World-Changer, the 19th of 21 galactic archetypes. All 21 archetypes are rooted in the Hunab Ku, the galactic core where the storehouse of the universal mind and memory resides.

The fifth force oracle of the Blue Lunar Storm year (including the planets and archetypes) is as follows:

The Worldchanger (Storm/SP Pluto) is guided by the Magician (Monkey/SP Venus); supported by the Enlightened One (Sun/GK Pluto); challenged/strengthened by the Healer (Moon/GK Mercury), and receives hidden help from the Spirit Essence/High Priestess (Wind/GK Uranus).

The world-changing Storm opens the third matrix portal in the Court of Hunab Ku. The stars, including our sun, are the receivers of the streams of life and knowledge emitted by the Hunab Ku, also known as the "One Giver of Movement and Measure."

The Storm exemplifies energy and self-generation as the love of Hunab Ku. This may be the most powerful year we have experienced since the inception of the New Sirius Cycle. The key theme is to let go of all preconceptions and let the Storm of Change sweep through and transfigure you. The Lunar Storm reminds us to remain in our center as the winds of change whip in all directions. From our Center, we may embody the Hunab Ku, the Source of all life and knowledge throughout world systems.

The Day Out of Time, Blue Lunar Night, Kin 223 (GK Saturn), is the sign of the stabilization of the spiritual abundance of the higher dream. Let's dream and manifest a world of equality, where all beings are fortified with the necessary abundance of Mother Nature so that they can unimpedely follow their bliss, awaken their connection with their star family, rediscover their healing powers and live a life filled with love, art and unity in harmony.

Stephanie South
Red Electric Serpent
Red Queen
Foundation for the Law of Time

LIVE FROM THE INSIDE OUT
RATHER THAN FROM THE OUTSIDE IN.

# RAINBOW BRIDGE MEDITATION

Before the meditation it is good to take a few moments to clear your mind, dissolving all thoughts as they arise. Also focus on feeling love arise in your heart. When you feel your mind clear, then begin the visualisation.

Visualise yourself inside the Earth's octahedron crystal core. Feel your heart at the center of this crystal core generating an intensely blazing point of white light.

This light from your heart core creates an etheric column that extends to the North and South poles from the blazing center to the tips of the octahedron.

Now visualize a great stream of multicolored plasma-filled light emanating from your heart core and flowing along the central axis toward both of Earth's poles, shooting out from them, to become two rainbow bands, 180 degrees apart.

As Earth revolves on its axis, this rainbow bridge remains steady and constant, unmoving. Feel the two streams of rainbow light rushing through your central column, shooting out from above your head and beneath your feet to create a Rainbow Bridge around your body.

Now you and the Rainbow Bridge are one. The Rainbow Bridge of world peace is real. Visualised by enough people in a telepathic wave of love, the Rainbow Bridge will become a reality.

lawoftime.org/rainbowbridge

# 13 MOON CALENDAR

The coming new era on our planet has everything to do with a change of timing frequency. The 13 Moon-28-day calendar is a simple tool that helps us to raise our frequency and gives us a new lens to view both our day-to-day and planetary events.

Because both Gregorian and 13 Moon calendars operate with 52 7-day weeks annually (364 days), the 13 Moon calendar provides a perfect daily transition tool for hooking back up with the higher-dimensional order! It is simple to bridge and follow day-to-day, as it is marked with the Gregorian dates.

The 13 Moon calendar is comprised of elegantly simple cycles. Namely: The 7-day week and 28-day moon. Unlike the Gregorian calendar, the days of the moon (month) and the days of the week line up perfectly, week-to-week and moon-to-moon. This makes the 13 Moon/28-day a perpetual calendar.

**Month 1** •

| 1 | 2 | 3 | 4 | 5 | 6 | 7 |
|---|---|---|---|---|---|---|
| 8 | 9 | 10 | 11 | 12 | 13 | 14 |
| 15 | 16 | 17 | 18 | 19 | 20 | 21 |
| 22 | 23 | 24 | 25 | 26 | 27 | 28 |

**Month 2** ••

| 1 | 2 | 3 | 4 | 5 | 6 | 7 |
|---|---|---|---|---|---|---|
| 8 | 9 | 10 | 11 | 12 | 13 | 14 |
| 15 | 16 | 17 | 18 | 19 | 20 | 21 |
| 22 | 23 | 24 | 25 | 26 | 27 | 28 |

**Month 3** •••

| 1 | 2 | 3 | 4 | 5 | 6 | 7 |
|---|---|---|---|---|---|---|
| 8 | 9 | 10 | 11 | 12 | 13 | 14 |
| 15 | 16 | 17 | 18 | 19 | 20 | 21 |
| 22 | 23 | 24 | 25 | 26 | 27 | 28 |

**Month 4** ••••

| 1 | 2 | 3 | 4 | 5 | 6 | 7 |
|---|---|---|---|---|---|---|
| 8 | 9 | 10 | 11 | 12 | 13 | 14 |
| 15 | 16 | 17 | 18 | 19 | 20 | 21 |
| 22 | 23 | 24 | 25 | 26 | 27 | 28 |

**Month 5** —

| 1 | 2 | 3 | 4 | 5 | 6 | 7 |
|---|---|---|---|---|---|---|
| 8 | 9 | 10 | 11 | 12 | 13 | 14 |
| 15 | 16 | 17 | 18 | 19 | 20 | 21 |
| 22 | 23 | 24 | 25 | 26 | 27 | 28 |

**Month 6**

| 1 | 2 | 3 | 4 | 5 | 6 | 7 |
|---|---|---|---|---|---|---|
| 8 | 9 | 10 | 11 | 12 | 13 | 14 |
| 15 | 16 | 17 | 18 | 19 | 20 | 21 |
| 22 | 23 | 24 | 25 | 26 | 27 | 28 |

**Month 7**

| 1 | 2 | 3 | 4 | 5 | 6 | 7 |
|---|---|---|---|---|---|---|
| 8 | 9 | 10 | 11 | 12 | 13 | 14 |
| 15 | 16 | 17 | 18 | 19 | 20 | 21 |
| 22 | 23 | 24 | 25 | 26 | 27 | 28 |

**Month 8**

| 1 | 2 | 3 | 4 | 5 | 6 | 7 |
|---|---|---|---|---|---|---|
| 8 | 9 | 10 | 11 | 12 | 13 | 14 |
| 15 | 16 | 17 | 18 | 19 | 20 | 21 |
| 22 | 23 | 24 | 25 | 26 | 27 | 28 |

**Month 9**

| 1 | 2 | 3 | 4 | 5 | 6 | 7 |
|---|---|---|---|---|---|---|
| 8 | 9 | 10 | 11 | 12 | 13 | 14 |
| 15 | 16 | 17 | 18 | 19 | 20 | 21 |
| 22 | 23 | 24 | 25 | 26 | 27 | 28 |

**Month 10**

| 1 | 2 | 3 | 4 | 5 | 6 | 7 |
|---|---|---|---|---|---|---|
| 8 | 9 | 10 | 11 | 12 | 13 | 14 |
| 15 | 16 | 17 | 18 | 19 | 20 | 21 |
| 22 | 23 | 24 | 25 | 26 | 27 | 28 |

**Month 11**

| 1 | 2 | 3 | 4 | 5 | 6 | 7 |
|---|---|---|---|---|---|---|
| 8 | 9 | 10 | 11 | 12 | 13 | 14 |
| 15 | 16 | 17 | 18 | 19 | 20 | 21 |
| 22 | 23 | 24 | 25 | 26 | 27 | 28 |

**Month 12**

| 1 | 2 | 3 | 4 | 5 | 6 | 7 |
|---|---|---|---|---|---|---|
| 8 | 9 | 10 | 11 | 12 | 13 | 14 |
| 15 | 16 | 17 | 18 | 19 | 20 | 21 |
| 22 | 23 | 24 | 25 | 26 | 27 | 28 |

**Month 13**

| 1 | 2 | 3 | 4 | 5 | 6 | 7 |
|---|---|---|---|---|---|---|
| 8 | 9 | 10 | 11 | 12 | 13 | 14 |
| 15 | 16 | 17 | 18 | 19 | 20 | 21 |
| 22 | 23 | 24 | 25 | 26 | 27 | 28 |

# 13 MOON PLANETARY SERVICE WAVESPELL

**MAGNETIC MOON**
What is my purpose?

**LUNAR MOON**
What is my challenge?

**ELECTRIC MOON**
How can I best serve?

**SELFEXISTING MOON**
What is the form of action?

**OVERTONE MOON**
How to empower myself?

13 Moons of 28 days = 364 days
+ 1 Day Out of Time = 365 days
of the Earth around the Sun

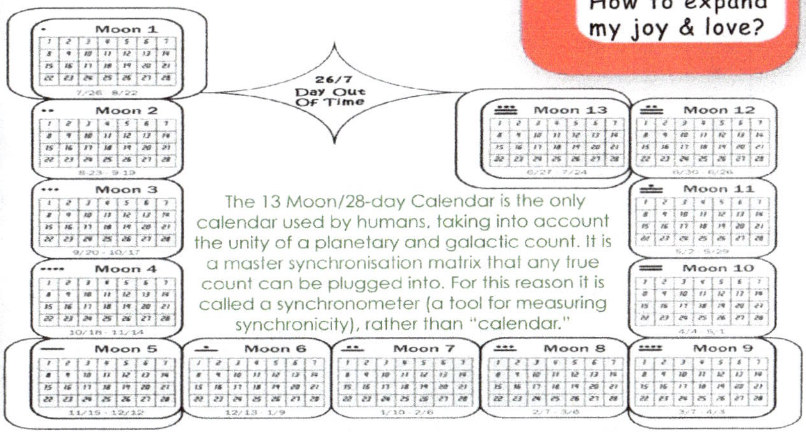


The 13 Moon/28-day Calendar is the only calendar used by humans, taking into account the unity of a planetary and galactic count. It is a master synchronisation matrix that any true count can be plugged into. For this reason it is called a synchronometer (a tool for measuring synchronicity), rather than "calendar."

**COSMIC MOON**
How to expand my joy & love?

**CRYSTAL MOON**
Discuss past & future action

**SPECTRAL MOON**
How do I release and let go?

**PLANETARY MOON**
How do I perfect what I do?

**RHYTHMIC MOON**
Gather Resources

**RESONANT MOON**
Attune service to others

**GALACTIC MOON**
Do I live what I believe?

**SOLAR MOON**
How do I attain purpose?

# 20 SOLAR TRIBES

| # | GLYPH | MAYA NAME | ACTION | ESSENCE | TIME CELL | POWER |
|---|---|---|---|---|---|---|
| 1 |  | DRAGON IMIX | NURTURES | BEING | INPUT | BIRTH |
| 2 |  | WIND IK | COMMUNICATES | BREATH | INPUT | SPIRIT |
| 3 |  | NIGHT AKBAL | DREAMS | INTUITION | INPUT | ABUNDANCE |
| 4 |  | SEED KAN | TARGETS | AWARENESS | INPUT | FLOWERING |
| 5 |  | SERPENT CHICCHAN | SURVIVES | INSTINCT | STORE | LIFE FORCE |
| 6 |  | WORLDBRIDGER CIMI | EQUALISES | OPPORTUNITY | STORE | DEATH |
| 7 |  | HAND MANIK | KNOWS | HEALING | STORE | ACCOMPLISHMENT |
| 8 |  | STAR LAMAT | BEAUTIFIES | ART | STORE | ELEGANCE |
| 9 |  | MOON MULUC | PURIFIES | FLOW | PROCESS | UNIVERSAL WATER |
| 10 |  | DOG OC | LOVES | LOYALTY | PROCESS | HEART |
| 11 |  | MONKEY CHUEN | PLAYS | ILLUSION | PROCESS | MAGIC |
| 12 |  | HUMAN EB | INFLUENCES | WISDOM | PROCESS | FREE WILL |
| 13 |  | SKYWALKER BEN | EXPLORES | WAKEFULNESS | OUTPUT | SPACE |
| 14 |  | WIZARD IX | ENCHANTS | RECEPTIVITY | OUTPUT | TIMELESSNESS |
| 15 |  | EAGLE MEN | CREATES | MIND | OUTPUT | VISION |
| 16 |  | WARRIOR CIB | QUESTIONS | FEARLESSNESS | OUTPUT | INTELLIGENCE |
| 17 |  | EARTH CABAN | EVOLVES | SYNCHRONICITY | MATRIX | NAVIGATION |
| 18 |  | MIRROR ETZNAB | REFLECTS | ORDER | MATRIX | ENDLESSNESS |
| 19 |  | STORM CAUAC | CATALYSES | ENERGY | MATRIX | SELF GENERATION |
| 0/20 |  | SUN AHAU | ENLIGHTENS | LIFE | MATRIX | UNIVERSAL FIRE |

# 13 GALACTIC TONES

| TONE | NAME | MAYA | POWER | ACTION | ESSENCE | PULSE OF EXPERIENCE |
|---|---|---|---|---|---|---|
| • | MAGNETIC | HUN | UNIFY | ATTRACT | PURPOSE | TIME (SPIRITUAL) |
| •• | LUNAR | CA | POLARISE | STABILISE | CHALLENGE | LIFE (PHYSICAL) |
| ••• | ELECTRIC | OX | ACTIVATE | BOND | SERVICE | SENSE (EMOTIONAL) |
| •••• | SELFEXISTING | CAN | DEFINE | MEASURE | FORM | MIND (MENTAL) |
| ▬ | OVERTONE | HO | EMPOWER | COMMAND | RADIANCE | TIME |
| • ▬ | RHYTHMIC | UAC | ORGANISE | BALANCE | EQUALITY | LIFE |
| •• ▬ | RESONANT | UC | CHANNEL | INSPIRE | ATTUNEMENT | SENSE |
| ••• ▬ | GALACTIC | OAXAC | HARMONISE | MODEL | INTEGRITY | MIND |
| •••• ▬ | SOLAR | BOLON | PULSE | REALISE | INTENTION | TIME |
| ▬ ▬ | PLANETARY | LAHUN | PERFECT | PRODUCE | MANIFESTATION | LIFE |
| • ▬ ▬ | SPECTRAL | HUN LAHUN | DISSOLVE | RELEASE | LIBERATION | SENSE |
| •• ▬ ▬ | CRYSTAL | CA LAHUN | DEDICATE | UNIVERSALISE | COOPERATION | MIND |
| ••• ▬ ▬ | COSMIC | OX LAHUN | ENDURE | TRANSCEND | PRESENCE | TIME |

I tone power in order to tribe action
Tone actioning tribe essence
I seal the time cell of tribe power
With the tone name tone of tone essence
I am guided by the power of guide tribe power

If the day is a galactic portal day add
I am a Galactic Activation Portal, enter me!

# TZOLKIN - COUNT OF DAYS/LIGHT
# 13:20 HARMONIC MATRIX

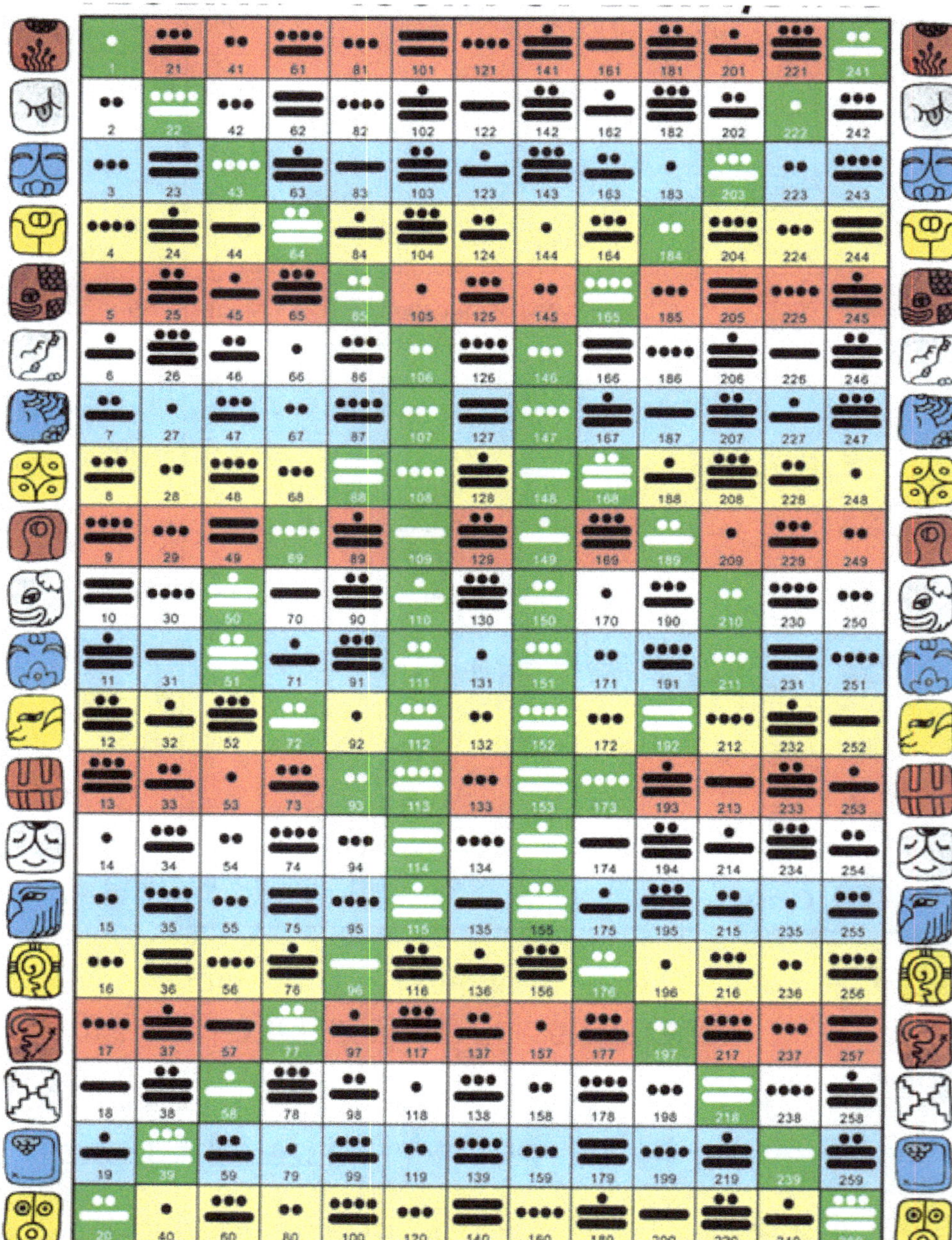

# FIND YOUR GALACTIC SIGNATURE

*Your Galactic Signature is your portal into fourth-dimensional time.*

To find your Signature:

1. Find your Birth Year Number on the chart to the right and your Month Number from below.
2. Add those two numbers to the Day Number of the month you were born.
3. If greater than 260, subtract 260. This is the Kin Number on the Tzolkin on the opposite page.
4. Note the Tone on the Tzolkin and follow horizontally along the row to find your Tribe.

Voila, your GALACTIC SIGNATURE
Welcome to the New Time!
Eg: 26/7/2020
26 + 181 (July) + 172 (2020) = 379
379 - 260 = 119
KIN 119 - BLUE LUNAR STORM

| Gregorian Month You Were Born | | | | | |
|---|---|---|---|---|---|
| January | 0 | May | 120 | September | 243 |
| February | 31 | June | 151 | October | 13 |
| March | 59 | July | 181 | November | 44 |
| April | 90 | August | 212 | December | 74 |

| BIRTH YEAR | | | # |
|---|---|---|---|
| 2065 | 2013 | 1961 | 217 |
| 2064 | 2012 | 1960 | 112 |
| 2063 | 2011 | 1959 | 7 |
| 2062 | 2010 | 1958 | 162 |
| 2061 | 2009 | 1957 | 57 |
| 2060 | 2008 | 1956 | 212 |
| 2059 | 2007 | 1955 | 107 |
| 2058 | 2006 | 1954 | 2 |
| 2057 | 2005 | 1953 | 157 |
| 2056 | 2004 | 1952 | 52 |
| 2055 | 2003 | 1951 | 207 |
| 2054 | 2002 | 1950 | 102 |
| 2053 | 2001 | 1949 | 257 |
| 2052 | 2000 | 1948 | 152 |
| 2051 | 1999 | 1947 | 47 |
| 2050 | 1998 | 1946 | 202 |
| 2049 | 1997 | 1945 | 97 |
| 2048 | 1996 | 1944 | 252 |
| 2047 | 1995 | 1943 | 147 |
| 2046 | 1994 | 1942 | 42 |
| 2045 | 1993 | 1941 | 197 |
| 2044 | 1992 | 1940 | 92 |
| 2043 | 1991 | 1939 | 247 |
| 2042 | 1990 | 1938 | 142 |
| 2041 | 1989 | 1937 | 37 |
| 2040 | 1988 | 1936 | 192 |
| 2039 | 1987 | 1935 | 87 |
| 2038 | 1986 | 1934 | 242 |
| 2037 | 1985 | 1933 | 137 |
| 2036 | 1984 | 1932 | 32 |
| 2035 | 1983 | 1931 | 187 |
| 2034 | 1982 | 1930 | 82 |
| 2033 | 1981 | 1929 | 237 |
| 2032 | 1980 | 1928 | 132 |
| 2031 | 1979 | 1927 | 27 |
| 2030 | 1978 | 1926 | 182 |
| 2029 | 1977 | 1925 | 77 |
| 2028 | 1976 | 1924 | 232 |
| 2027 | 1975 | 1923 | 127 |
| 2026 | 1974 | 1922 | 22 |
| 2025 | 1973 | 1921 | 177 |
| 2024 | 1972 | 1920 | 72 |
| 2023 | 1971 | 1919 | 227 |
| 2022 | 1970 | 1918 | 122 |
| 2021 | 1969 | 1917 | 17 |
| 2020 | 1968 | 1916 | 172 |
| 2019 | 1967 | 1915 | 67 |
| 2018 | 1966 | 1914 | 222 |
| 2017 | 1965 | 1913 | 117 |
| 2016 | 1964 | 1912 | 12 |
| 2015 | 1963 | 1911 | 167 |
| 2014 | 1962 | 1910 | 62 |

## YOUR FOUNDATION
# ◈ ORACLE & WAVESPELL

**Create your Foundation Oracle & Wavespell**

1. Find your Signature from your Birth date on Pg 11. Insert your Signature in the central box above.
2. Build your Oracle by following instructions on Pg 20.
3. Find your Signature on the Tzolkin on Pg 10. Insert the 13-Day Cycle or Wavespell.

Enjoy jumping deeper, exploring your LIFE's evolutionary journey!

## YOUR CURRENT YEAR

# ORACLE & WAVESPELL

**Create this Years Oracle & Wavespell**
Follow same steps as for Foundation Oracle & Wavespell (opposite page), only this time adding your Birth Day and Month to **this** Year. Revealing your **YEAR's** evolution!
You will find the Glyph will be from the horizontal alighnment of your Earth Family on pg 13 - **Planet Art Holon**.
If your age is a multiple of 4, it will be your foundation Glyph.

# LUNAR GARDENING

To garden by the moon choose both the correct phase of the moon firstly and then the most beneficial sign for any action or inaction!

Take into account seasonal changes of weather. Go organic.

New Moon, 1st quarter
Above ground crops. Begin new projects

2nd quarter Above ground crops.
Nurture & tend to new growth

Full Moon, 3rd quarter - Root crops.
finish off projects & tasks. Harvest

4th quarter - Begin compost heaps & worm farms. Remove noxious growth weeds and pests. Harvest. Rest

| SIGNS | CROPS | OTHER ACTIVITIES |
|---|---|---|
| ♈ Aries | None | Cultivating, weeding, destroying pests, harvesting |
| ♉ Taurus | Root crops, especially potatoes & bulbous plants; flowers for hardiness, beans, cabbage, hay, lettuce, onion sets, radish, turnip, leafy vegetables. Peach, pear and plum trees. | General maintenance |
| ♊ Gemini | None | Cultivating, weeding, destroying noxious growth & pests, harvesting mow lawns to retard growth. |
| ♋ Cancer | Planting reliable seeds and transplanting should produce good results. Asparagus, barley, beets, berries, bulbs, carrots, corn, lettuce, potatoes, roses, herbs, wheat, deciduous trees. | Irrigation; bud and graft. |
| ♌ Leo | None | Destroy weeds and noxious growth/pests. Deaden trees. Mow lawns to retard growth, harvesting |
| ♍ Virgo | Plant flowers & vines. Don't plant vegetables or trees. | Cultivation, destroy weeds etc.. |
| ♎ Libra | Seeds for hay, corn, fodder, grain. Flowers for beauty, bulbs. Barley, beans, beet, cabbage, carrot, peas, squash, tubers, vines | Cultivate, weed |
| ♏ Scorpio | Beans, berries, cantaloupes, cauliflower, cereal, chicory, eggplant (aubergine), peas, potatoes, pumpkin. Flowers for abundance. | Do not dig potatoes! Sturdiness is a special quality of Scorpio |
| ♐ Sagittarius | Onion (seeds), endive, leeks, garlic, peppers, radish, potatoes, European trees such as oak. | Harvesting, destroying weeds. |
| ♑ Capricorn | Bulbs, potatoes, root crops, beans, cabbage, broccoli, lettuce, onion sets, radish. Flowers for hardiness. Fruit trees | General maintenance |
| ♒ Aquarius | Absolutely not. | Cultivation, extermination, harvesting |
| ♓ Pisces | Broccoli, bulbs, Brussels sprouts, carrot, celery, cress, chicory, cucumber, endive, horseradish, parsley, peanuts, radish, pumpkin. Flowers for abundance. Deciduous trees. | Compost heaps started in the fourth quarter under ♋ will be amazing (worm farms too)! |

Moon Cycles

# RED WEEK INITIATE

Red Week One - Magnetic Bat Moon: Knowledge Initiates View - Claim Power of Prophecy

Dali 1/7

WHITE WIZARD WAVESPELL 14
Power of Timelessness

*Kiche count (see below)* — 7 Lamat (Kiche Count)

White Magnetic Wizard

Kin: 14

*Moon and Planets signs* — ☉♌, ☾♉, ☿♋℞, ♀♋, ♂♌, ♃♐ ℞, ♄♑℞, ♅♉, ♆♓℞, ♇♑℞, ⚷♈℞, ☊♋

*Radial Plasma - day of the week*

*Day & Moon*

DRAGON GENESIS - Power of Dreaming(130-days)
RED EASTERN CASTLE OF TURNING (52-days)
Court of Birth: Initiate Seed, Power of Entering
WHITE GALACTIC SPECTRUM (65-days)
Dog Season of Heart
(1) *'The one who knows' (20-day Vinals - Wizard days this year)*

*Gregorian date* — Fri 26/7

Seli 2/7

*Oracles (pg 16)*

*Vinals*

☾♊6.29pm

Blue Lunar Eagle

Kin: 15

**All times are given in NZ time = GMT + 14 hrs**
**To convert for Australia: NSW, VIC minus 2 hrs;**
**QLD minus 2 hrs (check daylight savings; SA/NT minus 2½ hrs;**
**WA, Indonesia minus 4 hrs**
**Check daylight savings differences at www.worldtimezone.com**

## other Symbols

Galactic Activation Portal
GAP day

Pacal Votan Clear Sign

*This page assists to read the day pages ahead.*

The Ki'che or Long Count is the Mayan Calendar followed in Guatemala through generations. It speaks of the Guatemala Maya and their stories throughout time, representing their Earth walk.

It compliments the Dreamspell Count of Palenque, (held in stone for 1260 years). Representing the Galactic Walk, with branches grounded in the Earth, reaching to the heavens, the evolutionary path.

Approached this way, without the need to choose one or the other , we receive the full benefit of the Tzolkin - Sacred Count of Days. This deep wisdom has been prepared for this time of most need - whether passed through humans or held in stone...

For more on the Ki'che Count www.SacredRoad.org
www.lawoftime.org & www.timewaves.org for Dreamspell Count

# 13 MOON SYNCHRONOMETER – 1ST MOON OF BLUE LUNAR STORM YEAR

| DALI SUNDAY | SELI MONDAY | GAMMA TUESDAY | KALI WEDNESDAY | ALPHA THURSDAY | LIMI FRIDAY | SILIO SATURDAY |
|---|---|---|---|---|---|---|
| 119 JUL 26 BLUE LUNAR STORM **1** | 120 JUL 27 YELLOW ELECTRIC SUN **2** | 121 JUL 28 RED SELF-EXISTING DRAGON **3** | 122 JUL 29 WHITE OVERTONE WIND **4** | 123 JUL 30 BLUE RHYTHMIC NIGHT **5** | 124 JUL 31 YELLOW RESONANT SEED **6** | 125 AUG 1 RED GALACTIC SERPENT **7** |
| 126 AUG 2 WHITE SOLAR WORLDBRIDGER **8** | 127 AUG 3 BLUE PLANETARY HAND **9** | 128 AUG 4 YELLOW SPECTRAL STAR ○ **10** | 129 AUG 5 RED CRYSTAL MOON **11** | 130 AUG 6 WHITE COSMIC DOG **12** | 131 AUG 7 BLUE MAGNETIC MONKEY **13** | 132 AUG 8 YELLOW LUNAR HUMAN **14** |
| 133 AUG 9 RED ELECTRIC SKYWALKER **15** | 134 AUG 10 WHITE SELF-EXISTING WIZARD **16** | 135 AUG 11 BLUE OVERTONE EAGLE **17** | 136 AUG 12 YELLOW RHYTHMIC WARRIOR **18** | 137 AUG 13 RED RESONANT EARTH **19** | 138 AUG 14 WHITE GALACTIC MIRROR **20** | 139 AUG 15 BLUE SOLAR STORM **21** |
| 140 AUG 16 YELLOW PLANETARY SUN **22** | 141 AUG 17 RED SPECTRAL DRAGON **23** | 142 AUG 18 WHITE CRYSTAL WIND **24** | 143 AUG 19 BLUE COSMIC NIGHT ● **25** | 144 AUG 20 YELLOW MAGNETIC SEED **26** | 145 AUG 21 RED LUNAR SERPENT **27** | 146 AUG 22 WHITE ELECTRIC WORLDBRIDGER **28** |

MAGNETIC BAT MOON ● What Is My Purpose?

She was centred and calm, the eye of the storm around her.
More then ever the world required stillness,
for only in that void of emptiness could she hear the worlds whispers
like owls wings rustling through leaves.
Time had ceased, crumpled and collapsed upon itself along with all constructed realities.
All that remained, the eternal beating heart of the earth,
ancient metronome, rhythmic reminder keeping track of the seasons.
She no longer remembered what it was to be seperate or even to want,
for the warmth that flowed through her now was contentment and life itself.
It was strange to think of eons spent searching, etching paths across oceans in search for stillness.
She returned home defeated and weary, to realise she was trying to master the obsolete.
Planting seeds in concrete would never yield fruit.
Some feared isolation not knowing it was fertile ground for cultivation.
Weaving dreams, that trickled from her like light on mycelium networks
connecting all those who dreamed new into being, she had found her place

DEEP LISTENING

Heidi Holland
IG thou.art.revolution

# RED WEEK INITIATE

Red Week One - Magnetic Bat Moon: Knowledge Initiates View - Claim Power of Prophecy

Dali 1/7

9 Ix (Kl'che Count)
☉♋, ☾♍, ☿♊
♀♉, ♂♓, ♃♐ ℞
♄♑℞, ♅♈, ♆♒℞
♇♐℞, ⚷♓℞, ☊♊℞

Blue Lunar Storm

Kin: 119

DRAGON GENESIS - Power of Dreaming (130-days)
BLUE WESTERN CASTLE OF BURNING (52-days)
Court of Magic: Transform Star, Power of Turning Around
BLUE GALACTIC SPECTRUM (65-days)
Eagle Season of Vision
*(1) 'The one who knows' (20-day Vinals - every Storm day this year)*

Sun 26/7

Seli 2/7

☾♎6.20am

Yellow Electric Sun

Kin: 120

YELLOW GALACTIC SPECTRUM (65-days)
Sun Season of Universal Fire

Mon 27/7

Gamma 3/7

☊♊D12.25am

Red Self-Existing Dragon

Kin: 121

Tue 28/7

Kali 4/7

☾♏9.19am

White Overtone Wind

Kin: 122

Wed 29/7

# MOON OF PURPOSE

Alpha 5/7

Blue Rhythmic Night

Kin: 123

Thu 30/7

1 Cauac

☾♐1.36pm

☊♊℞ 9.32pm

Limi 6/7

Yellow Resonant Seed

Kin: 124

Fri 31/7

♀♊11.41am

Silio 7/7

Red Galactic Serpent

Kin: 125

Sat 1/8

# WHITE WEEK REFINE

White Week Two - Magnetic Bat Moon: Humility Refines Meditation - Maintain Power of Prophecy

Dali 8/7

☿♋10.04am
☾♑7.27pm

White Solar World-Bridger

Kin: 126

Sun 2/8

Seli 9/7

Blue Planetary Hand

Kin: 127

Mon 3/8

Gamma 10/7

○ 3.58am

Yellow Spectral Star

Kin: 128

Tue 4/8

Kali 11/7

☾♒3.18am

Red Crystal Moon

Kin: 129

Wed 5/8

# MOON OF PURPOSE

Alpha 12/7

White Cosmic Dog

Kin: 130

DRAGON GENESIS COMPLETE
Turning Around Occurs

Thu 6/8

BLUE MONKEY WAVESPELL 11
Power of Magic

☾♊ 1.28pm

Limi 13/7

Blue Magnetic Monkey

Kin: 131

Fri 7/8

MONKEY GENESIS - Power of Magic (Kins 131-208/78-days)

Silio 14/7

Yellow Lunar Human

Kin: 132

Sat 8/8

Week 2/13

# BLUE WEEK TRANSFORM

Blue Week Three - Magnetic Bat Moon: Patience Transforms Conduct - Maintain Power of Prophecy

Dali 15/7

Red Electric Skywalker

Kin: 133

Sun 9/8

☾♈1.37am

Seli 16/7

White Self-Existing Wizard

Kin: 134

Mon 10/8

☾♑4.51pm

Gamma 17/7

Blue Overtone Eagle

Kin: 135

Tue 11/8

☾♉2.07pm

Kali 18/7

Yellow Rhythmic Warrior

Kin: 136

Wed 12/8

# MOON OF PURPOSE

Alpha 19/7

Red Resonant Earth

Kin: 137

Thu 13/8

1 Eb

Limi 20/7

White Galactic Mirror

Kin: 138

Fri 14/8

☾♊12.35am

Silio 21/7

Blue Solar Storm

Kin: 139

Sat 15/8 *(2) 'Listens in Silence'*

Week 3/13

# YELLOW WEEK RIPEN

Yellow Week Four - Magnetic Bat Moon: Power Ripens Fruit - Become Victory of Prophecy

**Dali** 22/7

♅℞ 12.35am

Yellow Planetary Sun

Kin: 140

Sun 16/8

**Seli** 23/7

♂ ♈ 12.59am
☉♌ 1.42am
☽♋ 7.23am
☿♌ 2.59pm

Red Spectral Dragon

Kin: 141

Mon 17/8

**Gamma** 24/7

White Crystal Wind

Kin: 142

Tue 18/8

**Kali** 25/7

☽♌ 10.39am
● 2.41pm

Blue Cosmic Night

Kin: 143

Wed 19/8

# MOON OF PURPOSE

YELLOW SEED WAVESPELL 4
Power of Flowering

Alpha 26/7

Yellow Magnetic Seed

Kin: 144

Thu 20/8

☾♍11.46am

Limi 27/7

Red Lunar Serpent

Kin: 145

Fri 21/8

Silio 28/7

White Electric World-Bridger

Kin: 146

Sat 22/8

Week 4/13

# 13 MOON SYNCHRONOMETER - 2ND MOON OF BLUE LUNAR STORM YEAR

| DALI SUNDAY | SELI MONDAY | GAMMA TUESDAY | KALI WEDNESDAY | ALPHA THURSDAY | LIMI FRIDAY | SILIO SATURDAY |
|---|---|---|---|---|---|---|
| 147 AUG 23 BLUE SELF-EXISTING HAND **1** | 148 AUG 24 YELLOW OVERTONE STAR **2** | 149 AUG 25 RED RHYTMIC MOON **3** | 150 AUG 26 WHITE RESONANT DOG **4** | 151 AUG 27 BLUE GALACTIC MONKEY **5** | 152 AUG 28 YELLOW SOLAR HUMAN **6** | 153 AUG 29 RED PLANETARY SKYWALKER **7** |
| 154 AUG 30 WHITE SPECTRAL WIZARD **8** | 155 AUG 31 BLUE CRYSTAL EAGLE **9** | 156 SEP 1 YELLOW COSMIC WARRIOR **10** | 157 SEP 2 RED MAGNETIC EARTH **11** | 158 SEP 3 WHITE LUNAR MIRROR **12** | 159 SEP 4 BLUE ELECTRIC STORM **13** | 160 SEP 5 YELLOW SELF-EXISTING SUN **14** |
| 161 SEP 6 RED OVERTONE DRAGON **15** | 162 SEP 7 WHITE RHYTMIC WIND **16** | 163 SEP 8 BLUE RESONANT NIGHT **17** | 164 SEP 9 YELLOW GALACTIC SEED **18** | 165 SEP 10 RED SOLAR SERPENT **19** | 166 SEP 11 WHITE PLANETARY WORLDBRIDGER **20** | 167 SEP 12 BLUE SPECTRAL HAND **21** |
| 168 SEP 13 YELLOW CRYSTAL STAR **22** | 169 SEP 14 RED COSMIC MOON **23** | 170 SEP 15 WHITE MAGNETIC DOG **24** | 171 SEP 16 BLUE LUNAR MONKEY **25** | 172 SEP 17 YELLOW ELECTRIC HUMAN **26** | 173 SEP 18 RED SELF-EXISTING SKYWALKER **27** | 174 SEP 19 WHITE OVERTONE WIZARD **28** |

LUNAR SCORPION MOON

What Is My Challenge?

LOVING COMPASSION
www.izzyivyart.com

Izzy Ivy
IG izzy_ivy_art
FB izzyivyart

# RED WEEK INITIATE

Red Week One - Lunar Scorpion Moon: Knowledge Initiates View - Claim Power of Prophecy

**Dali** 1/2 ☾♎12.37pm

Blue Self-Existing Hand

Kin: 147

Sun 23/8

**Seli** 2/2

Yellow Overtone Star

Kin: 148

Mon 24/8

**Gamma** 3/2 ☾♏2.47pm

Red Rhythmic Moon

Kin: 149

Tue 25/8

**Kali** 4/2 1 Chicchan

White Resonant Dog

Kin: 150

Wed 26/8

MOON OF
# CHALLENGE

☾♐7.08pm

Alpha 5/2

Blue Galactic Monkey

Kin: 151

Thu 27/8

Limi 6/2

Yellow Solar Human

Kin: 152

Fri 28/8

Silio 7/2

Red Planetary Skywalker

Kin: 153

Sat 29/8

# WHITE WEEK REFINE

White Week Two - Lunar Scorpion Moon: Humility Refines Meditation - Maintain Power of Prophecy

Dali 8/2

☾♑1.43am

White Spectral Wizard

Kin: 154

Sun 30/8

Seli 9/2

Blue Crystal Eagle

Kin: 155

Mon 31/8

Gamma 10/2

♀♋8.34am
☾♒10.19am

Yellow Cosmic Warrior

Kin: 156

FATHERS DAY

Tue 1/9

Kali 11/2

RED EARTH WAVESPELL 17
Power of Navigation

○5.21pm
☿♍6.33pm

Red Magnetic Earth

Kin: 157

YELLOW SOUTHERN CASTLE OF GIVING (Kins 157-208/52-days)
Court of Intelligenc Court of Intelligence: Ripen Sun

Wed 2/9

# MOON OF CHALLENGE

☾♓8.45pm

Alpha 12/2

White Lunar Mirror

Kin: 158

WHITE NORTHERN CASTLE OF CROSSING (Kins 53-104 /52-days)
Court of Death: Refine Warrior, Power of Descending

Thu 3/9

Limi 13/2

Blue Electric Storm

Kin: 159

Fri 4/9 *(3) 'In order to integrate the Universe'*

Silio 14/2

Yellow Self-Existing Sun

Kin: 160

BLUE GALACTIC SPECTRUM (Kins 55-119/65-days)
Eagle Season of Vision

Sat 5/9

# BLUE WEEK TRANSFORM

Blue Week Three - Lunar Scorpion Moon: Patience Transforms Conduct - Maintain Power of Prophecy

Dali 15/2

☾♈8.52am

Red Overtone Dragon

Kin: 161

Sun 6/9

Seli 16/2

White Rhythmic Wind

Kin: 162

Mon 7/9

Gamma 17/2

1 ETZNAB

☾♉9.40pm

Blue Resonant Night

Kin: 163

Tue 8/9

Kali 18/2

Yellow Galactic Seed

Kin: 164

Wed 9/9

# MOON OF CHALLENGE

♂R℞ 10.19am

Alpha 19/2

Red Solar Serpent

Kin: 165

Thu 10/9

☾♊ 9.08am

Limi 20/2

White Planetary World-Bridger

Kin: 166

Fri 11/9

Silio 21/2

Blue Spectral Hand

Kin: 167

Sat 12/9

Yellow Week Four - Lunar Scorpion Moon: Power Ripens Fruit - Become Victory of Prophecy

Dali 22/2

♃D1.05pm
☽♋5.07pm

Yellow Crystal Star
Kin: 168

Sun 13/9

Seli 23/2

Red Cosmic Moon
Kin: 169

Mon 14/9

Gamma 24/2

WHITE DOG WAVESPELL 10
Power of Heart

☽♌8.56pm

White Magnetic Dog
Kin: 170

Tue 15/9

Kali 25/2

Blue Lunar Monkey
Kin: 171

Wed 16/9

## MOON OF CHALLENGE

☉♍1.38am
☽♍9.38pm
●11pm

Alpha 26/2

Yellow Electric Human

Kin: 172

Thu 17/9

Limi 27/2

Red Self-Existing Skywalker

Kin: 173

Fri 18/9

☽♎9.13pm

Silio 28/2

White Overtone Wizard

Kin: 174

Sat 19/9

Week 8/13

# 13 MOON SYNCHRONOMETER - 3RD MOON OF BLUE LUNAR STORM YEAR

| DALI<br>SUNDAY | SELI<br>MONDAY | GAMMA<br>TUESDAY | KALI<br>WEDNESDAY | ALPHA<br>THURSDAY | LIMI<br>FRIDAY | SILIO<br>SATURDAY |
|---|---|---|---|---|---|---|
| 175 SEP 20<br>BLUE RHYTMIC EAGLE<br>1 | 176 SEP 21<br>YELLOW RESONANT WARRIOR<br>2 | 177 SEP 22<br>RED GALACTIC EARTH<br>3 | 178 SEP 23<br>WHITE SOLAR MIRROR<br>4 | 179 SEP 24<br>BLUE PLANETARY STORM<br>5 | 180 SEP 25<br>YELLOW SPECTRAL SUN<br>6 | 181 SEP 26<br>RED CRYSTAL DRAGON<br>7 |
| 182 SEP 27<br>WHITE COSMIC WIND<br>8 | 183 SEP 28<br>BLUE MAGNETIC NIGHT<br>9 | 184 SEP 29<br>YELLOW LUNAR SEED<br>10 | 185 SEP 30<br>RED ELECTRIC SERPENT<br>11 | 186 OCT 1<br>WHITE SELF-EXISTING WORLDBRIDGER<br>12 | 187 OCT 2<br>BLUE OVERTONE HAND<br>○ 13 | 188 OCT 3<br>YELLOW RHYTMIC STAR<br>14 |
| 189 OCT 4<br>RED RESONANT MOON<br>15 | 190 OCT 5<br>WHITE GALACTIC DOG<br>16 | 191 OCT 6<br>BLUE SOLAR MONKEY<br>17 | 192 OCT 7<br>YELLOW PLANETARY HUMAN<br>18 | 193 OCT 8<br>RED SPECTRAL SKYWALKER<br>19 | 194 OCT 9<br>WHITE CRYSTAL WIZARD<br>20 | 195 OCT 10<br>BLUE COSMIC EAGLE<br>21 |
| 196 OCT 11<br>YELLOW MAGNETIC WARRIOR<br>22 | 197 OCT 12<br>RED LUNAR EARTH<br>23 | 198 OCT 13<br>WHITE ELECTRIC MIRROR<br>24 | 199 OCT 14<br>BLUE SELF-EXISTING STORM<br>25 | 200 OCT 15<br>YELLOW OVERTONE SUN<br>26 | 201 OCT 16<br>RED RHYTMIC DRAGON<br>27 | 202 OCT 17<br>WHITE RESONANT WIND<br>● 28 |

ELECTRIC DEER MOON

●●● How can I best Serve?

UNDER THE BODHI TREE

Heidi Holland
IG thou.art.revolution

# RED WEEK INITIATE

Red Week One - Electric Deer Moon: Knowledge Initiates View - Claim Power of Prophecy

Dali 1/3 ☊♉3.54am

Blue Rhythmic Eagle

Kin: 175

Sun 20/9

Seli 2/3

1 CHUEN

☾♏9.47pm

Yellow Resonant Warrior

Kin: 176

Mon 21/9

Gamma 3/3 ☿♎11.23pm

Red Galactic Earth

Kin: 177

Tue 22/9

Kali 4/3

White Solar Mirror

Kin: 178

EQUINOX

Wed 23/9

MOON OF
# SERVICE

☾♐12.55am

Alpha 5/3

Blue Planetary Storm

Kin: 179

Thu 24/9

*(4) 'Based on knowledge'*

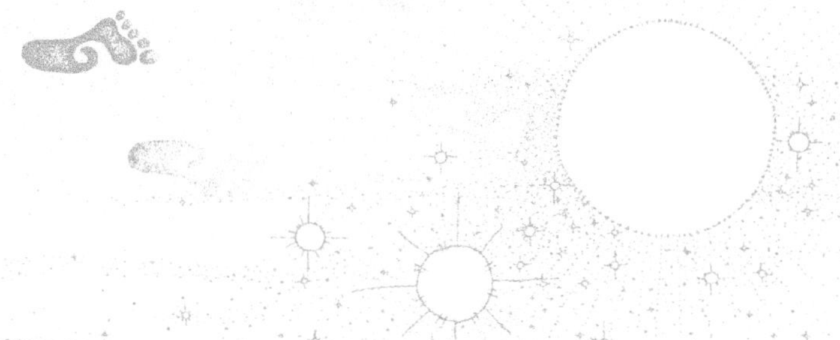

Limi 6/3

Yellow Spectral Sun

Kin: 180

Fri 25/9

☾♑7.12am

Silio 7/3

Red Crystal Dragon

Kin: 181

Sat 26/9

Week 9/13

# WHITE WEEK
# REFINE

White Week Two - Electric Deer Moon: Humility Refines Meditation - Maintain Power of Prophecy

Dali 8/3 ☾♒5.12pm

White Cosmic Wind

Kin: 182

Sun 27/9

Seli 9/3

BLUE NIGHT WAVESPELL 3
Power of Abundance

♀♌8.34am

Blue Magnetic Night

Kin: 183

Daylight Savings begins NZ +1 hour

Mon 28/9

Gamma 10/3 ♄D6.19pm

Yellow Lunar Seed

Kin: 184

Tue 29/9

Kali 11/3

Red Electric Serpent

Kin: 185

RED GALACTIC SPECTRUM (Kins 185-249/65-days)
Serpent Season of Life Force

Wed 30/9

# MOON OF SERVICE

○ 4.07am

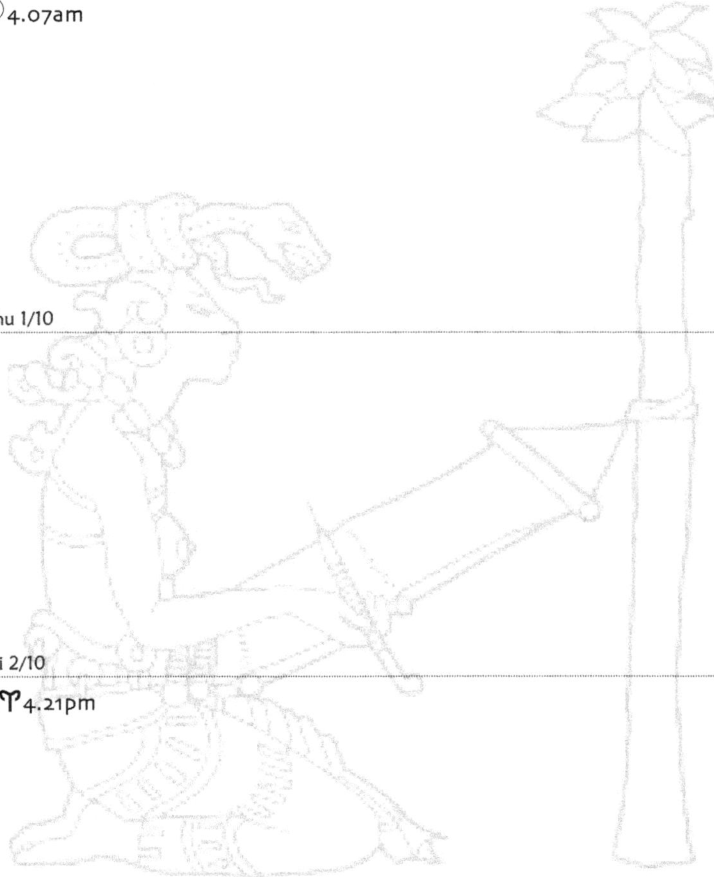

Alpha 12/3

White Self-Existing World-Bridger

Kin: 186

Thu 1/10

Limi 13/3

Blue Overtone Hand

Kin: 187

Fri 2/10

☾♈ 4.21pm

Silio 14/3

Yellow Rhythmic Star

Kin: 188

Sat 3/10

# BLUE WEEK TRANSFORM

Blue Week Three - Electric Deer Moon: Patience Transforms Conduct - Maintain Power of Prophecy

Dali 15/3

1 Kan

♂♅(℞)5.39pm

Red Resonant Moon

Kin: 189

Sun 4/10

Seli 16/3

♇ D

White Galactic Dog

Kin: 190

Daylight Savings begins NSW, Vic, Tas, SA, ACT +1 hour

Mon 5/10

Gamma 17/3

☽♉5.12am

Blue Solar Monkey

Kin: 191

Tue 6/10

Kali 18/3

Yellow Planetary Human

Kin: 192

Wed 7/10

# MOON OF SERVICE

☾♊ 5.17pm

Alpha 19/3

Red Spectral Skywalker

Kin: 193

Thu 8/10

Limi 20/3

White Crystal Wizard

Kin: 194

Fri 9/10

Silio 21/3

Blue Cosmic Eagle

Kin: 195

Sat 10/10

Yellow Week Four - Electric Deer Moon: Power Ripens Fruit - Become Victory of Prophecy

Dali 22/3

YELLOW WARRIOR WAVESPELL 16
Power of Intelligence

☾♋2.40am

Yellow Magnetic Warrior

Kin: 196

Sun 11/10

Seli 23/3

Red Lunar Earth

Kin: 197

Mon 12/10

Gamma 24/3

☾♌8am

White Electric Mirror

Kin: 198

Tue 13/10

Kali 25/3

☿℞ 2.05pm

Blue Self-Existing Storm

Kin: 199

*(5) 'That reaches the foundations'*

Wed 14/10

MOON OF
# SERVICE

☾♍9.33am

Alpha 26/3

Yellow Overtone Sun

Kin: 200

Thu 15/10

Limi 27/3

Red Rhythmic Dragon

Kin: 201

Fri 16/10

●8.30am

☾♎8.55am

Silio 28/3

White Resonant Wind

Kin: 202

Sat 17/10

Week 12/13

# 13 MOON SYNCHRONOMETER - 4TH MOON OF BLUE LUNAR STORM YEAR

| DALI SUNDAY | SELI MONDAY | GAMMA TUESDAY | KALI WEDNESDAY | ALPHA THURSDAY | LIMI FRIDAY | SILIO SATURDAY |
|---|---|---|---|---|---|---|
| 203 OCT 18 BLUE GALACTIC NIGHT **1** | 204 OCT 19 YELLOW SOLAR SEED **2** | 205 OCT 20 RED PLANETARY SERPENT **3** | 206 OCT 21 WHITE SPECTRAL WORLDBRIDGER **4** | 207 OCT 22 BLUE CRYSTAL HAND **5** | 208 OCT 23 YELLOW COSMIC STAR **6** | 209 OCT 24 RED MAGNETIC MOON **7** |
| 210 OCT 25 WHITE LUNAR DOG **8** | 211 OCT 26 BLUE ELECTRIC MONKEY **9** | 212 OCT 27 YELLOW SELF-EXISTING HUMAN **10** | 213 OCT 28 RED OVERTONE SKYWALKER **11** | 214 OCT 29 WHITE RHYTMIC WIZARD **12** | 215 OCT 30 BLUE RESONANT EAGLE **13** | 216 OCT 31 YELLOW GALACTIC WARRIOR **14** |
| 217 NOV 1 RED SOLAR EARTH ○ **15** | 218 NOV 2 WHITE PLANETARY MIRROR **16** | 219 NOV 3 BLUE SPECTRAL STORM **17** | 220 NOV 4 YELLOW CRYSTAL SUN **18** | 221 NOV 5 RED COSMIC DRAGON **19** | 222 NOV 6 WHITE MAGNETIC WIND **20** | 223 NOV 7 BLUE LUNAR NIGHT **21** |
| 224 NOV 8 YELLOW ELECTRIC SEED **22** | 225 NOV 9 RED SELF-EXISTING SERPENT **23** | 226 NOV 10 WHITE OVERTONE WORLDBRIDGER **24** | 227 NOV 11 BLUE RHYTMIC HAND **25** | 228 NOV 12 YELLOW RESONANT STAR **26** | 229 NOV 13 RED GALACTIC MOON **27** | 230 NOV 14 WHITE SOLAR DOG **28** |

**SELFEXISTING OWL MOON** ●●●● **What is the Form of my Service?**

ANCIENT EYES

Hannah Vela
www.hannahvela.com

# RED WEEK INITIATE

Red Week One - Self-existing Owl Moon: Knowledge Initiates View - Claim Power of Prophecy

Dali 1/4

Blue Galactic Night

Kin: 203

Sun 18/10

Seli 2/4

☾♏ 8.17am

Yellow Solar Seed

Kin: 204

Mon 19/10

Gamma 3/4

Red Planetary Serpent

Kin: 205

Tue 20/10

Kali 4/4

☾♐ 9.43am

White Spectral World-Bridger

Kin: 206

Wed 21/10

# MOON OF FORM

Alpha 5/4

Blue Crystal Hand

Kin: 207

Thu 22/10

☾♑2.32pm
♀♍6.16pm

Limi 6/4

Yellow Cosmic Star

Kin: 208

Fri 23/10 MONKEY GENESIS COMPLETE

RED MOON WAVESPELL 9
Power of Universal Water

Silio 7/4

Red Magnetic Moon

Kin: 209

MOON GENESIS - Power of Magical Flight (Kins 209-260/52-days)
GREEN CENTRAL CASTLE OF ENCHANTMENT (Kins 209-260/52-days)
Court of th Matrix : Synchronise Human

Sat 24/10

# WHITE WEEK
# REFINE

White Week Two - Self-existing Owl Moon: Humility Refines Meditation - Maintain Power of Prophecy

**Dali** 8/4 — ☾♒10.57pm

White Lunar Dog

Kin: 210

BLUE WESTERN CASTLE OF BURNING (Kins 105-156/52-days)
Court of Magic: Transform Star, Power of Turning Around — Sun 25/10

**Seli** 9/4

Blue Electric Monkey

Kin: 211

Mon 26/10

**Gamma** 10/4

Yellow Self-Existing Human

Kin: 212

Tue 27/10

**Kali** 11/4 — ☾♓10.01am

Red Overtone Skywalker

Kin: 213

Wed 28/10

MOON OF
# FORM

Alpha 12/4

White Rhythmic Wizard

Kin: 214

Thu 29/10

Limi 13/4

1 Oc

☾♈10.28pm

Blue Resonant Eagle

Kin: 215

Fri 30/10

Silio 14/4

Yellow Galactic Warrior

Kin: 216

Sat 31/10

**BELTAINE**

Week 1/13

Blue Week Three - Self-existing Owl Moon: Patience Transforms Conduct - Maintain Power of Prophecy

**Dali** 15/4 ○3.48am

Red Solar Earth

Kin: 217

Sun 1/11

**Seli** 16/4 ☾♉11.11am

White Planetary Mirror

Kin: 218

Mon 2/11

**Gamma** 17/4

Blue Spectral Storm

Kin: 219

*(6) 'Where with great wisdom a seed is sown'* Tue 3/11

**Kali** 18/4 ☿D6.51am ☾♊11.15pm

Yellow Crystal Sun

Kin: 220

Wed 4/11

# MOON OF FORM

Alpha 19/4

Red Cosmic Dragon

Kin: 221

Thu 5/11 GUY FAWKES NIGHT

WHITE WIND WAVESPELL 2

Power of Spirit

Limi 20/4

White Magnetic Wind

Kin: 222

Fri 6/11

☾♋9.19am

Silio 21/4

Blue Lunar Night

Kin: 223

Sat 7/11

Week 2/13

# YELLOW WEEK
# RIPEN

Yellow Week Four - Self-existing Owl Moon: Power Ripens Fruit - Become Victory of Prophecy

Dali 22/4

Yellow Electric Seed

Kin: 224

Sun 8/11

Seli 23/4

☾♌4.13pm

Red Self-Existing Serpent

Kin: 225

Mon 9/11

Gamma 24/4

White Overtone World-Bridger

Kin: 226

Tue 10/11

Kali 25/4

☾♍7.31pm

Blue Rhythmic Hand

Kin: 227

Wed 11/11

MOON OF
# FORM

1 Akbal

Alpha 26/4

Yellow Resonant Star

Kin: 228

Thu 12/11

☾♎8.02pm

Limi 27/4

Red Galactic Moon

Kin: 229

Fri 13/11

♂D1.40pm

Silio 28/4

White Solar Dog

Kin: 230

Sat 14/11

Week 3/13

# 13 MOON SYNCHRONOMETER - 5TH MOON OF BLUE LUNAR STORM YEAR

| DALI SUNDAY | SELI MONDAY | GAMMA TUESDAY | KALI WEDNESDAY | ALPHA THURSDAY | LIMI FRIDAY | SILIO SATURDAY |
|---|---|---|---|---|---|---|
| 231 NOV 15 BLUE PLANETARY MONKEY 1 | 232 NOV 16 YELLOW SPECTRAL HUMAN 2 | 233 NOV 17 RED CRYSTAL SKYWALKER 3 | 234 NOV 18 WHITE COSMIC WIZARD 4 | 235 NOV 19 BLUE MAGNETIC EAGLE 5 | 236 NOV 20 YELLOW LUNAR WARRIOR 6 | 237 NOV 21 RED ELECTRIC EARTH 7 |
| 238 NOV 22 WHITE SELF-EXISTING MIRROR 8 | 239 NOV 23 BLUE OVERTONE STORM 9 | 240 NOV 24 YELLOW RHYTMIC SUN 10 | 241 NOV 25 RED RESONANT DRAGON 11 | 242 NOV 26 WHITE GALACTIC WIND 12 | 243 NOV 27 BLUE SOLAR NIGHT 13 | 244 NOV 28 YELLOW PLANETARY SEED 14 |
| 245 NOV 29 RED SPECTRAL SERPENT 15 | 246 NOV 30 WHITE CRYSTAL WORLDBRIDGER 16 | 247 DEC 1 BLUE COSMIC HAND 17 | 248 DEC 2 YELLOW MAGNETIC STAR 18 | 249 DEC 3 RED LUNAR MOON 19 | 250 DEC 4 WHITE ELECTRIC DOG 20 | 251 DEC 5 BLUE SELF-EXISTING MONKEY 21 |
| 252 DEC 6 YELLOW OVERTONE HUMAN 22 | 253 DEC 7 RED RHYTMIC SKYWALKER 23 | 254 DEC 8 WHITE RESONANT WIZARD 24 | 255 DEC 9 BLUE GALACTIC EAGLE 25 | 256 DEC 10 YELLOW SOLAR WARRIOR 26 | 257 DEC 11 RED PLANETARY EARTH 27 | 258 DEC 12 WHITE SPECTRAL MIRROR 28 |

**OVERTONE PEACOCK MOON — How can I best Empower myself?**

PEACE WITHIN THE CHAOS

Fiona Craig
FB Fiona Jane Craig

# RED WEEK INITIATE

Red Week One - Overtone Peacock Moon: Knowledge Initiates View - Claim Power of Prophecy

**Dali** 1/5

● 6.06pm
☾♏ 7.29pm

Blue Planetary Monkey

Kin: 231

Sun 15/11

**Seli** 2/5

☉♏ 2.24pm

Yellow Spectral Human

Kin: 232

Mon 16/11

**Gamma** 3/5

♀♎ 8.33am
☾♐ 7.52pm

Red Crystal Skywalker

Kin: 233

Tue 17/11

**Kali** 4/5

White Cosmic Wizard

Kin: 234

Wed 18/11

# MOON OF RADIANCE

BLUE EAGLE WAVESPELL 15
Power of Vision

☾♑11.01pm

Alpha 5/5

Blue Magnetic Eagle

Kin: 235

Thu 19/11

♃♑8.54pm

Limi 6/5

Yellow Lunar Warrior

Kin: 236

Fri 20/11

Silio 7/5

Red Electric Earth

Kin: 237

Sat 21/11

Week 4/13

# WHITE WEEK
# REFINE

White Week Two - Overtone Peacock Moon: Humility Refines Meditation - Maintain Power of Prophecy

Dali 8/5 ☾♒5.56am

White Self-Existing Mirror

Kin: 238

Sun 22/11

Seli 9/5

Blue Overtone Storm

Kin: 239

(7) 'A little ray of the hidden sun'

Mon 23/11

Gamma 10/5 ☾♓4.23pm

Yellow Rhythmic Sun

Kin: 240

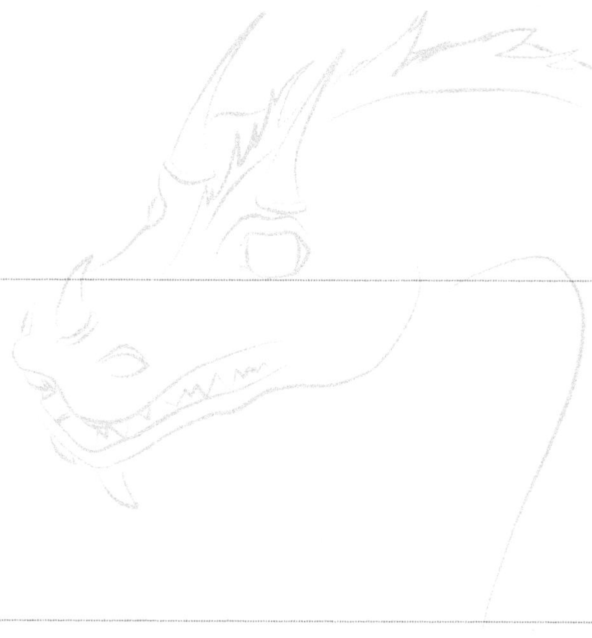

Tue 24/11

Kali 11/5

1 Cib

Red Resonant Dragon

Kin: 241

Wed 25/11

# MOON OF RADIANCE

Alpha 12/5

White Galactic Wind

Kin: 242

Thu 26/11

☾♈ 4.51am

Limi 13/5

Blue Solar Night

Kin: 243

Fri 27/11

Silio 14/5

Yellow Planetary Seed

Kin: 244

Sat 28/11

Week 5/13

# BLUE WEEK TRANSFORM

Blue Week Three - Overtone Peacock Moon: Patience Transforms Conduct - Maintain Power of Prophecy

Dali 15/5

♆D3.35pm
☾♉5.32pm

Red Spectral Serpent

Kin: 245

Sun 29/11

Seli 16/5

○10.29pm
☍ Penumbral Lunar Eclipse

White Crystal World-Bridger

Kin: 246

Mon 30/11

Gamma 17/5

Blue Cosmic Hand

Kin: 247

Tue 1/12

Kali 18/5

YELLOW STAR WAVESPELL 8
Power of Elegance

☾♊5.07am

Yellow Magnetic Star

Kin: 248

Wed 2/12

# MOON OF RADIANCE

Alpha 19/5

Red Lunar Moon

Kin: 249

Thu 3/12

☾♋2.53pm

Limi 20/5

White Electric Dog

Kin: 250

WHITE GALACTIC SPECTRUM (Kin 250-54/65-days)
Dog Season fo Heart

Fri 4/12

Silio 21/5

Blue Self-Existing Monkey

Kin: 251

Sat 5/12

Week 6/13

# YELLOW WEEK RIPEN

Yellow Week Four - Overtone Peacock Moon: Power Ripens Fruit - Become Victory of Prophecy

**Dali** *22/5* ☾♌10.16pm

Yellow Overtone Human

Kin: 252

Sun 6/12

**Seli** *23/5*

Red Rhythmic Skywalker

Kin: 253

Mon 7/12

**Gamma** *24/5* 1 Muluc

White Resonant Wizard

Kin: 254

Tue 8/12

**Kali** *25/5* ☾♍3.02am

Blue Galactic Eagle

Kin: 255

Wed 9/12

# MOON OF RADIANCE

Alpha 26/5

Yellow Solar Warrior

Kin: 256

Thu 10/12

Limi 27/5

☾♎5.23am
♀♏12.48pm

Red Planetary Earth

Kin: 257

Fri 11/12

Silio 28/5

White Spectral Mirror

Kin: 258

Sat 12/12

# 13 MOON SYNCHRONOMETER - 6TH MOON OF BLUE LUNAR STORM YEAR

| DALI SUNDAY | SELI MONDAY | GAMMA TUESDAY | KALI WEDNESDAY | ALPHA THURSDAY | LIMI FRIDAY | SILIO SATURDAY |
|---|---|---|---|---|---|---|
| 259 DEC 13<br>BLUE CRYSTAL STORM<br>1 | 260 DEC 14<br>YELLOW COSMIC SUN<br>2 | 1 DEC 15<br>RED MAGNETIC DRAGON<br>3 | 2 DEC 16<br>WHITE LUNAR WIND<br>4 | 3 DEC 17<br>BLUE ELECTRIC NIGHT<br>5 | 4 DEC 18<br>YELLOW SELF-EXISTING SEED<br>6 | 5 DEC 19<br>RED OVERTONE SERPENT<br>7 |
| 6 DEC 20<br>WHITE RHYTMIC WORLDBRIDGER<br>8 | 7 DEC 21<br>BLUE RESONANT HAND<br>9 | 8 DEC 22<br>YELLOW GALACTIC STAR<br>10 | 9 DEC 23<br>RED SOLAR MOON<br>11 | 10 DEC 24<br>WHITE PLANETARY DOG<br>12 | 11 DEC 25<br>BLUE SPECTRAL MONKEY<br>13 | 12 DEC 26<br>YELLOW CRYSTAL HUMAN<br>14 |
| 13 DEC 27<br>RED COSMIC SKYWALKER<br>15 | 14 DEC 28<br>WHITE MAGNETIC WIZARD<br>16 | 15 DEC 29<br>BLUE LUNAR EAGLE<br>17 | 16 DEC 30<br>YELLOW ELECTRIC WARRIOR<br>18 | 17 DEC 31<br>RED SELF-EXISTING EARTH<br>19 | 18 JAN 1<br>WHITE OVERTONE MIRROR<br>20 | 19 JAN 2<br>BLUE RHYTMIC STORM<br>21 |
| 20 JAN 3<br>YELLOW RESONANT SUN<br>22 | 21 JAN 4<br>RED GALACTIC DRAGON<br>23 | 22 JAN 5<br>WHITE SOLAR WIND<br>24 | 23 JAN 6<br>BLUE PLANETARY NIGHT<br>25 | 24 JAN 7<br>YELLOW SPECTRAL SEED<br>26 | 25 JAN 8<br>RED CRYSTAL SERPENT<br>27 | 26 JAN 9<br>WHITE COSMIC WORLDBRIDGER<br>28 |

RHYTHMIC LIZARD MOON  How can I Organise for Equality?

SIRIUS ACTIVATION

Dennis Mandala
www.sirius-arts.com

# RED WEEK INITIATE

Red Week One - Rhytmic Lizard Moon: Knowledge Initiates View - Claim Power of Prophecy

Dali 1/6 ☾♏6.12am

Blue Crystal Storm

Kin: 259

(8) *'Which unifies all of the pieces'* Sun 13/12

Seli 2/6

Yellow Cosmic Sun

Kin: 260

MAGICAL FLIGHT
MOON GENESIS COMPLETE
GALACTIC FREE WILL ATTAINED
Galactic Synchronisation

Mon 14/12

Gamma 3/6

RED DRAGON WAVESPELL 1
Power of Birth

●5.16am
☌Solar Eclipse
☾♐6.56am

Red Magnetic Dragon

Kin: 1

DRAGON GENESIS - Power of Dreaming (Kins 1-130/130-days)
RED EASTERN CASTLE OF TURNING (Kins 1-52/52-days)
Court of Birth: Initiate Seed, Power of Entering

Tue 15/12

Kali 4/6

☉♐5.03am
⚷D1.37pm

White Lunar Wind

Kin: 2

Wed 16/12

# MOON OF EQUALITY

☾♑9.18am

Alpha 5/6

Blue Electric Night

Kin: 3

Thu 17/12

Limi 6/6

Yellow Self-Existing Seed

Kin: 4

Fri 18/12

☾♒2.47pm

Silio 7/6

Red Overtone Serpent

Kin: 5

Sat 19/12

# WHITE WEEK REFINE

White Week Two - Rhytmic Lizard Moon: Humility Refines Meditation - Maintain Power of Prophecy

Dali 8/6

White Rhythmic World-Bridger

Sun 20/12

Seli 9/6

1 Ik

Blue Resonant Hand

SOLSTICE

Mon 21/12

Gamma 10/6

☾♓ 12am

Yellow Galactic Star

Tue 22/12

Kali 11/6

Red Solar Moon

Wed 23/12

# MOON OF EQUALITY

♂♈5.50pm
☾♈12.03pm

**Alpha** *12/6*

White Planetary Dog

Thu 24/12

**Limi** *13/6*

Blue Spectral Monkey

Fri 25/12

**Silio** *14/6*

Yellow Crystal Human

Sat 26/12

Week 9/13

# BLUE WEEK TRANSFORM

Blue Week Three - Rhytmic Lizard Moon: Patience Transforms Conduct - Maintain Power of Prophecy

Dali 15/6 ☾♉12.49am

Red Cosmic Skywalker

Kin: 13

Sun 27/12

Seli 16/6

WHITE WIZARD WAVESPELL 14
Power of Timelessness

White Magnetic Wizard

Kin: 14

Mon 28/12

Gamma 17/6 ☾♊12.10pm

Blue Lunar Eagle

Kin: 15

Tue 29/12

Kali 18/6 ○4.28pm

Yellow Electric Warrior

Kin: 16

Wed 30/12

# MOON OF EQUALITY

♇♑6.51am
☾♋9.09pm

Alpha 19/6

Red Self-Existing Earth

Kin: 17

Thu 31/12

Limi 20/6

White Overtone Mirror

Kin: 18

Fri 1/1

Silio 21/6

Blue Rhythmic Storm

Kin: 19

Sat 2/1 *(9) 'To enter into the well of inner wisdom'*

Week 10/13

# YELLOW WEEK RIPEN

Yellow Week Four - Rhytmic Lizard Moon: Power Ripens Fruit - Become Victory of Prophecy

Dali 22/6

1 Men
☾♌3,47am

Yellow Resonant Sun

Kin: 20

Sun 3/1

Seli 23/6

♀♐12.34pm

Red Galactic Dragon

Kin: 21

Mon 4/1

Gamma 24/6

☾♍8.35am
☿♑11.25am

White Solar Wind

Kin: 22

Tue 5/1

Kali 25/6

Blue Planetary Night

Kin: 23

Wed 6/1

# MOON OF EQUALITY

☾♎11.59am

Alpha 26/6

Yellow Spectral Seed

Kin: 24

Thu 7/1

Limi 27/6

Red Crystal Serpent

Kin: 25

Fri 8/1

☾♏2.28pm

Silio 28/6

White Cosmic World-Bridger

Kin: 26

Sat 9/1

# 13 MOON SYNCHRONOMETER - 7TH MOON OF BLUE LUNAR STORM YEAR

| DALI SUNDAY | SELI MONDAY | GAMMA TUESDAY | KALI WEDNESDAY | ALPHA THURSDAY | LIMI FRIDAY | SILIO SATURDAY |
|---|---|---|---|---|---|---|
| 27 JAN 10 BLUE MAGNETIC HAND **1** | 28 JAN 11 YELLOW LUNAR STAR **2** | 29 JAN 12 RED ELECTRIC MOON **3** | 30 JAN 13 WHITE SELF-EXISTING DOG ● **4** | 31 JAN 14 BLUE OVERTONE MONKEY **5** | 32 JAN 15 YELLOW RHYTMIC HUMAN **6** | 33 JAN 16 RED RESONANT SKYWALKER **7** |
| 34 JAN 17 WHITE GALACTIC WIZARD **8** | 35 JAN 18 BLUE SOLAR EAGLE **9** | 36 JAN 19 YELLOW PLANETARY WARRIOR **10** | 37 JAN 20 RED SPECTRAL EARTH **11** | 38 JAN 21 WHITE CRYSTAL MIRROR **12** | 39 JAN 22 BLUE COSMIC STORM **13** | 40 JAN 23 YELLOW MAGNETIC SUN **14** |
| 41 JAN 24 RED LUNAR DRAGON **15** | 42 JAN 25 WHITE ELECTRIC WIND **16** | 43 JAN 26 BLUE SELF-EXISTING NIGHT **17** | 44 JAN 27 YELLOW OVERTONE SEED **18** | 45 JAN 28 RED RHYTMIC SERPENT **19** | 46 JAN 29 WHITE RESONANT WORLDBRIDGER ○ **20** | 47 JAN 30 BLUE GALACTIC HAND **21** |
| 48 JAN 31 YELLOW SOLAR STAR **22** | 49 FEB 1 RED PLANETARY MOON **23** | 50 FEB 2 WHITE SPECTRAL DOG **24** | 51 FEB 3 BLUE CRYSTAL MONKEY **25** | 52 FEB 4 YELLOW COSMIC HUMAN **26** | 53 FEB 5 RED MAGNETIC SKYWALKER **27** | 54 FEB 6 WHITE LUNAR WIZARD **28** |

**RESONANT MONKEY MOON** How can I Attune my Service to Others?

INTENTION

Hope Medford
www.hopemedford.com

# RED WEEK INITIATE

Red Week One - Resonant Monkey Moon: Knowledge Initiates View - Claim Power of Prophecy

Dali 1/7

**BLUE HAND WAVESPELL 7**
Power of Accomplishment

Blue Magnetic Hand

Kin: 27

Sun 10/1

Seli 2/7

☾♐4.39pm

Yellow Lunar Star

Kin: 28

Mon 11/1

Gamma 3/7

Red Electric Moon

Kin: 29

Tue 12/1

Kali 4/7

●5.59pm
☾♑7.36pm

White Self-Existing Dog

Kin: 30

Wed 13/1

# MOON OF ATTUNEMENT

☉♑3.45pm
♅D1.16pm

Alpha 5/7

Blue Overtone Monkey

Kin: 31

Thu 14/1

Limi 6/7

Yellow Rhythmic Human

Kin: 32

Fri 15/1

1 Lamat
☽♒12.36am

Silio 7/7

Red Resonant Skywalker

Kin: 33

Sat 16/1

Week 12/13

# WHITE WEEK REFINE

White Week Two - Resonant Monkey Moon: Humility Refines Meditation - Maintain Power of Prophecy

Dali 8/7

White Galactic Wizard

Kin: 34

Sun 17/1

Seli 9/7

☾♓8.46am

Blue Solar Eagle

Kin: 35

Mon 18/1

Gamma 10/7

Yellow Planetary Warrior

Kin: 36

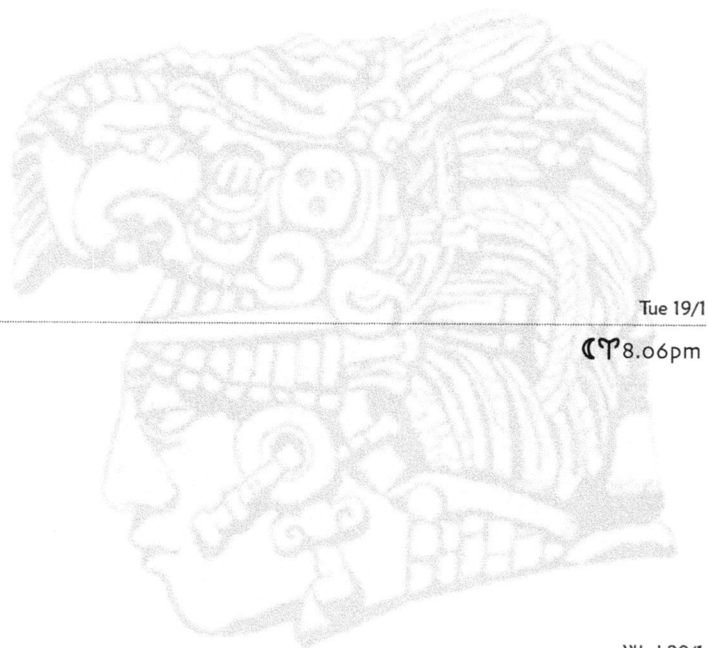

Tue 19/1

Kali 11/7

☾♈8.06pm

Red Spectral Earth

Kin: 37

Wed 20/1

# MOON OF ATTUNEMENT

(10) *'Where the student clears the mind, taking account of what is not yet ripe'*

Alpha 12/7

White Crystal Mirror

Thu 21/1

Limi 13/7

Blue Cosmic Storm

Fri 22/1

Silio 14/7

YELLOW SUN WAVESPELL ○
Power of Universal Fire

☾♉8.55am

Yellow Magnetic Sun

Sat 23/1

Week 13/13

Blue Week Three - Resonant Monkey Moon: Patience Transforms Conduct - Maintain Power of Prophecy

Dali 15/7

Red Lunar Dragon

Kin: 41

Sun 24/1

Seli 16/7

☾♊8.33pm
☿♒11.59pm

White Electric Wind

Kin: 42

Mon 25/1

Gamma 17/7

Blue Self-Existing Night

Kin: 43

Tue 26/1

Kali 18/7

Yellow Overtone Seed

Kin: 44

Wed 27/1

MOON OF
# ATTUNEMENT

☾♋5.13am
♀♑11am

Alpha 19/7

Red Rhythmic Serpent

Kin: 45

Thu 28/1

1 Imix
○8.19am

Limi 20/7

White Resonant World-Bridger

Kin: 46

Fri 29/1

☾♌10.51am

Silio 21/7

Blue Galactic Hand

Kin: 47

Sat 30/1

# YELLOW WEEK
# RIPEN

Yellow Week Four - Resonant Monkey Moon: Power Ripens Fruit - Become Victory of Prophecy

Dali 22/7 ☿℞4.52am

Yellow Solar Star

Kin: 48

Sun 31/1

Seli 23/7 ☽♍2.29pm

Red Planetary Moon

Kin: 49

LUGHNASADH Mon 1/2

Gamma 24/7

White Spectral Dog

Kin: 50

Tue 2/2

Kali 25/7 ☽♎5.20pm

Blue Crystal Monkey

Kin: 51

Wed 3/2

MOON OF
# ATTUNEMENT

Alpha 26/7

Yellow Cosmic Human

Kin: 52

Thu 4/2

RED SKYWALKER WAVESPELL 13
Power of Space

☿℞ ♑6.35am
☽♏8.17pm

Limi 27/7

Red Magnetic Skywalker

Kin: 53

WHITE NORTHERN CASTLE OF CROSSING (Kins 53-104/52-days)
Court of Death: Refine Warrior, Power of Descending

Fri 5/2

Silio 28/7

White Lunar Wizard

Kin: 54

Sat 6/2

Week 2/13

# 13 MOON SYNCHRONOMETER – 8TH MOON OF BLUE LUNAR STORM YEAR

| DALI SUNDAY | SELI MONDAY | GAMMA TUESDAY | KALI WEDNESDAY | ALPHA THURSDAY | LIMI FRIDAY | SILIO SATURDAY |
|---|---|---|---|---|---|---|
| 55 FEB 7 BLUE ELECTRIC EAGLE 1 | 56 FEB 8 YELLOW SELF-EXISTING WARRIOR 2 | 57 FEB 9 RED OVERTONE EARTH 3 | 58 FEB 10 WHITE RHYTMIC MIRROR 4 | 59 FEB 11 BLUE RESONANT STORM 5 | 60 FEB 12 YELLOW GALACTIC SUN ● 6 | 61 FEB 13 RED SOLAR DRAGON 7 |
| 62 FEB 14 WHITE PLANETARY WIND 8 | 63 FEB 15 BLUE SPECTRAL NIGHT 9 | 64 FEB 16 YELLOW CRYSTAL SEED 10 | 65 FEB 17 RED COSMIC SERPENT 11 | 66 FEB 18 WHITE MAGNETIC WORLDBRIDGER 12 | 67 FEB 19 BLUE LUNAR HAND 13 | 68 FEB 20 YELLOW ELECTRIC STAR 14 |
| 69 FEB 21 RED SELF-EXISTING MOON 15 | 70 FEB 22 WHITE OVERTONE DOG 16 | 71 FEB 23 BLUE RHYTMIC MONKEY 17 | 72 FEB 24 YELLOW RESONANT HUMAN 18 | 73 FEB 25 RED GALACTIC SKYWALKER 19 | 74 FEB 26 WHITE SOLAR WIZARD 20 | 75 FEB 27 BLUE PLANETARY EAGLE ○ 21 |
| 76 FEB 28 YELLOW SPECTRAL WARRIOR 22 | 77 MAR 1 RED CRYSTAL EARTH 23 | 78 MAR 2 WHITE COSMIC MIRROR 24 | 79 MAR 3 BLUE MAGNETIC STORM 25 | 80 MAR 4 YELLOW LUNAR SUN 26 | 81 MAR 5 RED ELECTRIC DRAGON 27 | 82 MAR 6 WHITE SELF-EXISTING WIND 28 |

GALACTIC HAWK MOON

Am I Walking my Talk?

REBIRTH

Stefani Mierzwa
IG @stefani.helena.art

# RED WEEK INITIATE

Red Week One - Galactic Hawk Moon: Knowledge Initiates View - Claim Power of Prophecy

**Dali** 1/8

☾♐11.45pm

Blue Electric Eagle

Kin: 55

BLUE GALACTIC SPRECTRUM (Kins 55-119/65-days)
Eagle Season of Vision

Sun 7/2

**Seli** 2/8

Yellow Self-Existing Warrior

Kin: 56

Mon 8/2

**Gamma** 3/8

Red Overtone Earth

Kin: 57

Tue 9/2

**Kali** 4/8

☾♑4am

White Rhythmic Mirror

Kin: 58

Wed 10/2

# MOON OF INTEGRITY

1 Ix

Alpha 5/8

Blue Resonant Storm

Kin: 59

Thu 11/2 *(11) 'Dissipating the clouds of doubt, raising her/himself up'*

●8.05am

☾♒9.41am

Limi 6/8

Yellow Galactic Sun

Kin: 60

Fri 12/2

☉♒4.42am

Silio 7/8

Red Solar Dragon

Kin: 61

Sat 13/2

White Week Two - Galactic Hawk Moon: Humility Refines Meditation - Maintain Power of Prophecy

Dali 8/8 ☾♓5.39pm

White Planetary Wind

Kin: 62

VALENTINES DAY Sun 14/2

Seli 9/8

Blue Spectral Night

Kin: 63

Mon 15/2

Gamma 10/8

Yellow Crystal Seed

Kin: 64

Tue 16/2

Kali 11/8 ☾♈4.27am

Red Cosmic Serpent

Kin: 65

Wed 17/2

# MOON OF INTEGRITY

WHITE WORLDBRIDGER WAVESPELL 6
Power of Death

Alpha 12/8

White Magnetic World-Bridger

Thu 18/2

☾♉5.11pm

Limi 13/8

Blue Lunar Hand

Fri 19/2

Silio 14/8

Yellow Electric Star

Sat 20/2

# BLUE WEEK TRANSFORM

Blue Week Three - Galactic Hawk Moon: Patience Transforms Conduct - Maintain Power of Prophecy

**Dali** *15/8*

♀♒9.53am
☿D1.53pm

Red Self-Existing Moon

Kin: 69

Sun 21/2

**Seli** *16/8*

☾♊5.25am
♂♉12.06pm

White Overtone Dog

Kin: 70

Mon 22/2

**Gamma** *17/8*

Blue Rhythmic Monkey

Kin: 71

Tue 23/2

**Kali** *18/8*

1 Manik
☾♋2.40pm

Yellow Resonant Human

Kin: 72

Wed 24/2

# MOON OF INTEGRITY

Alpha 19/8

Red Galactic Skywalker

Kin: 73

Thu 25/2

☾♌8.05pm

Limi 20/8

White Solar Wizard

Kin: 74

Fri 26/2

○9.17pm

Silio 21/8

Blue Planetary Eagle

Kin: 75

Sat 27/2

# YELLOW WEEK
# RIPEN

Yellow Week Four - Galactic Hawk Moon: Power Ripens Fruit - Become Victory of Prophecy

**Dali** 22/8

☾♍10.37pm

Yellow Spectral Warrior

Kin: 76

Sun 28/2

**Seli** 23/8

Red Crystal Earth

Kin: 77

Mon 1/3

**Gamma** 24/8

White Cosmic Mirror

Kin: 78

Tue 2/3

**Kali** 25/8

BLUE STORM WAVESPELL 19
Power of Self Generation

☾♎12am

Blue Magnetic Storm

Kin: 79

(12) *'Breaks with habitual caution and reaches the white light'*

Wed 3/3

# MOON OF INTEGRITY

Alpha 26/8

Yellow Lunar Sun

Kin: 80

Thu 4/3

☾♏ 1.50am

Limi 27/8

Red Electric Dragon

Kin: 81

Fri 5/3

Silio 28/8

White Self-Existing Wind

Kin: 82

Sat 6/3

Week 6/13

# 13 MOON SYNCHRONOMETER – 9TH MOON OF BLUE LUNAR STORM YEAR

| DALI SUNDAY | SELI MONDAY | GAMMA TUESDAY | KALI WEDNESDAY | ALPHA THURSDAY | LIMI FRIDAY | SILIO SATURDAY |
|---|---|---|---|---|---|---|
| 83 MAR 7 BLUE OVERTONE NIGHT **1** | 84 MAR 8 YELLOW RHYTMIC SEED **2** | 85 MAR 9 RED RESONANT SERPENT **3** | 86 MAR 10 WHITE GALACTIC WORLDBRIDGER **4** | 87 MAR 11 BLUE SOLAR HAND **5** | 88 MAR 12 YELLOW PLANETARY STAR **6** | 89 MAR 13 RED SPECTRAL MOON ● **7** |
| 90 MAR 14 WHITE CRYSTAL DOG **8** | 91 MAR 15 BLUE COSMIC MONKEY **9** | 92 MAR 16 YELLOW MAGNETIC HUMAN **10** | 93 MAR 17 RED LUNAR SKYWALKER **11** | 94 MAR 18 WHITE ELECTRIC WIZARD **12** | 95 MAR 19 BLUE SELF-EXISTING EAGLE **13** | 96 MAR 20 YELLOW OVERTONE WARRIOR **14** |
| 97 MAR 21 RED RHYTMIC EARTH **15** | 98 MAR 22 WHITE RESONANT MIRROR **16** | 99 MAR 23 BLUE GALACTIC STORM **17** | 100 MAR 24 YELLOW SOLAR SUN **18** | 101 MAR 25 RED PLANETARY DRAGON **19** | 102 MAR 26 WHITE SPECTRAL WIND **20** | 103 MAR 27 BLUE CRYSTAL NIGHT **21** |
| 104 MAR 28 YELLOW COSMIC SEED **22** | 105 MAR 29 RED MAGNETIC SERPENT ○ **23** | 106 MAR 30 WHITE LUNAR WORLDBRIDGER **24** | 107 MAR 31 BLUE ELECTRIC HAND **25** | 108 APR 1 YELLOW SELF-EXISTING STAR **26** | 109 APR 2 RED OVERTONE MOON **27** | 110 APR 3 WHITE RHYTMIC DOG **28** |

SOLAR JAGUAR MOON

How do I Realise my Purpose?

VIORIKA

Rich D'Amaru
IG @triplevisionintent

# RED WEEK INITIATE

Red Week One - Solar Jaguar Moon: Knowledge Initiates View - Claim Power of Prophecy

Dali 1/9

☾♐5.08am

Blue Overtone Night

Kin: 83

Sun 7/3

Seli 2/9

Yellow Rhythmic Seed

Kin: 84

Mon 8/3

Gamma 3/9

1 Ahau

☾♑10.09am

Red Resonant Serpent

Kin: 85

Tue 9/3

Kali 4/9

White Galactic World-Bridger

Kin: 86

Wed 10/3

# MOON OF INTENTION

☾♒4.51pm
☿♒8.05pm

Alpha 5/9

Blue Solar Hand

Kin: 87

Thu 11/3

Limi 6/9

Yellow Planetary Star

Kin: 88

Fri 12/3

●11.20pm

Silio 7/9

Red Spectral Moon

Kin: 89

Sat 13/3

White Week Two - Solar Jaguar Moon: Humility Refines Meditation - Maintain Power of Prophecy

Dali 8/9

☾♓1.27am

White Crystal Dog

Kin: 90

Sun 14/3

Seli 9/9

☉♓1.34am

Blue Cosmic Monkey

Kin: 91

Mon 15/3

Gamma 10/9

YELLOW HUMAN WAVESPELL 12
Power of Free Will

☾♈12.14pm

Yellow Magnetic Human

Kin: 92

Tue 16/3

Kali 11/9

♀♓10.31am

Red Lunar Skywalker

Kin: 93

ST PATRICK'S DAY

Wed 17/3

# MOON OF INTENTION

Alpha 12/9

White Electric Wizard

Kin: 94

Thu 18/3

☾♉12.52am

Limi 13/9

Blue Self-Existing Eagle

Kin: 95

Fri 19/3

Silio 14/9

Yellow Overtone Warrior

Kin: 96

Sat 20/3

EQUINOX

Week 8/13

Blue Week Three - Solar Jaguar Moon: Patience Transforms Conduct - Maintain Power of Prophecy

**Dali** 15/9 ☾♊1.39pm

Red Rhythmic Earth

Kin: 97

Sun 21/3

**Seli** 16/9 1 Ben

White Resonant Mirror

Kin: 98

Mon 22/3

**Gamma** 17/9

Blue Galactic Storm

Kin: 99

*(13) 'Closing the equivocating part and entering a trance'* Tue 23/3

**Kali** 18/9 ☾♋12.01am

Yellow Solar Sun

Kin: 100

Wed 24/3

MOON OF

# INTENTION

Alpha 19/9

Red Planetary Dragon

Kin: 101

Thu 25/3

☾♌ 6.19am

Limi 20/9

White Spectral Wind

Kin: 102

Fri 26/3

Silio 21/9

Blue Crystal Night

Kin: 103

Sat 27/3

Week 9/13

# YELLOW WEEK
# RIPEN

Yellow Week Four - Solar Jaguar Moon: Power Ripens Fruit - Become Victory of Prophecy

Dali 22/9

☾♍8.50am

Yellow Cosmic Seed

Kin: 104

Sun 28/3

Seli 23/9

RED SERPENT WAVESPELL 5
Power of Life Force

○7.47am

Red Magnetic Serpent

Kin: 105

BLUE WESTERN CASTLE OF BURNING (Kins 105-156/52-days)
Court of Magic: Transform Star: Power of Turning Around

Mon 29/3

Gamma 24/9

☾♎9.12am

White Lunar World-Bridger

Kin: 106

Tue 30/3

Kali 25/9

Blue Electric Hand

Kin: 107

Wed 31/3

MOON OF
# INTENTION

☿♓8.14am
☽♏9.26am

Alpha 26/9

Yellow Self-Existing Star

Kin: 108

Thu 1/4

Limi 27/9

Red Overtone Moon

Kin: 109

Fri 2/4

☽♐11.14am

Silio 28/9

White Rhythmic Dog

Kin: 110

Sat 3/4

Week 10/13

# 13 MOON SYNCHRONOMETER - 10TH MOON OF BLUE LUNAR STORM YEAR

| DALI SUNDAY | SELI MONDAY | GAMMA TUESDAY | KALI WEDNESDAY | ALPHA THURSDAY | LIMI FRIDAY | SILIO SATURDAY |
|---|---|---|---|---|---|---|
| 111 APR 4 BLUE RESONANT MONKEY **1** | 112 APR 5 YELLOW GALACTIC HUMAN **2** | 113 APR 6 RED SOLAR SKYWALKER **3** | 114 APR 7 WHITE PLANETARY WIZARD **4** | 115 APR 8 BLUE SPECTRAL EAGLE **5** | 116 APR 9 YELLOW CRYSTAL WARRIOR **6** | 117 APR 10 RED COSMIC EARTH **7** |
| 118 APR 11 WHITE MAGNETIC MIRROR **8** | 119 APR 12 BLUE LUNAR STORM ● **9** | 120 APR 13 YELLOW ELECTRIC SUN **10** | 121 APR 14 RED SELF-EXISTING DRAGON **11** | 122 APR 15 WHITE OVERTONE WIND **12** | 123 APR 16 BLUE RHYTMIC NIGHT **13** | 124 APR 17 YELLOW RESONANT SEED **14** |
| 125 APR 18 RED GALACTIC SERPENT **15** | 126 APR 19 WHITE SOLAR WORLDBRIDGER **16** | 127 APR 20 BLUE PLANETARY HAND **17** | 128 APR 21 YELLOW SPECTRAL STAR **18** | 129 APR 22 RED CRYSTAL MOON **19** | 130 APR 23 WHITE COSMIC DOG **20** | 131 APR 24 BLUE MAGNETIC MONKEY **21** |
| 132 APR 25 YELLOW LUNAR HUMAN **22** | 133 APR 26 RED ELECTRIC SKYWALKER **23** | 134 APR 27 WHITE SELF-EXISTING WIZARD ○ **24** | 135 APR 28 BLUE OVERTONE EAGLE **25** | 136 APR 29 YELLOW RHYTMIC WARRIOR **26** | 137 APR 30 RED RESONANT EARTH **27** | 138 MAY 1 WHITE GALACTIC MIRROR **28** |

**PLANETARY DOG MOON = How do I Perfect what I Do?**

GREEN TARA OF THE NEW EARTH

Kiri Ko
www.GypsYogini.me

# RED WEEK INITIATE

Red Week One - Planetary Dog Moon: Knowledge Initiates View - Claim Power of Prophecy

Dali 1/10 — 1 Cimi

Blue Resonant Monkey

Kin: 111

Sun 4/4

Seli 2/10 — ☾♑2.33pm

Yellow Galactic Human

Kin: 112

Daylight Savings ends NZ, NSW, Vic, Tas, SA, ACT --1 hour

Mon 5/4

Gamma 3/10 — ♃♒6.54am

Red Solar Skywalker

Kin: 113

Tue 6/4

Kali 4/10 — ☾♒9.30pm

White Planetary Wizard

Kin: 114

Wed 7/4

# MOON OF MANIFESTATION

Alpha 5/10

Blue Spectral Eagle

Kin: 115

Thu 8/4

Limi 6/10

Yellow Crystal Warrior

Kin: 116

Fri 9/4

☾♓6.47am
♀♈12.59pm

Silio 7/10

Red Cosmic Earth

Kin: 117

Sat 10/4

# WHITE WEEK
# REFINE

White Week Two - Planetary Dog Moon: Humility Refines Meditation - Maintain Power of Prophecy

Dali 8/10

WHITE MIRROR WAVESPELL 18
Power of Endlessness

White Magnetic Mirror

Kin: 118

Sun 11/4

Seli 9/10

● 2.30pm
☽♈ 6pm

Blue Lunar Storm

Kin: 119

*(14) 'Receives the light of one who knows'*

Mon 12/4

Gamma 10/10

Yellow Electric Sun

Kin: 120

YELLOW GALACTIC SPECTRUM (Kins 120-184/65-days)
Sun Season of Universal Fire)

Tue 13/4

Kali 11/10

♂♊ 7.44am
☉♈ 9.03am

Red Self-Existing Dragon

Kin: 121

Wed 14/4

# MOON OF MANIFESTATION

☾♉6.40am

Alpha 12/10

White Overtone Wind

Kin: 122

Thu 15/4

Limi 13/10

Blue Rhythmic Night

Kin: 123

Fri 16/4

1 Cauac

☿♈3.28am

☾♊7.39pm

Silio 14/10

Yellow Resonant Seed

Kin: 124

Sat 17/4

Week 12/13

# BLUE WEEK TRANSFORM

Blue Week Three - Planetary Dog Moon: Patience Transforms Conduct - Maintain Power of Prophecy

Dali 15/10

Red Galactic Serpent

Kin: 125

Sun 18/4

Seli 16/10

White Solar World-Bridger

Kin: 126

Mon 19/4

☾♋6.59am

Gamma 17/10

Blue Planetary Hand

Kin: 127

Tue 20/4

Kali 18/10

Yellow Spectral Star

Kin: 128

Wed 21/4

# MOON OF MANIFESTATION

☾♌2.45pm

Alpha 19/10

Red Crystal Moon

Kin: 129

Thu 22/4

Limi 20/10

White Cosmic Dog

Kin: 130

DRAGON GENESIS COMPLETE
Turning Around Occurs

Fri 23/4

BLUE MONKEY WAVESPELL 11
Power of Magic

☾♍6.26pm

Silio 21/10

Blue Magnetic Monkey

Kin: 131

Sat 24/4 MONKEY GENESIS - Power of Magic (Kins 131-208/78-days)

Week 13/13

# YELLOW WEEK
# RIPEN

Yellow Week Four - Planetary Dog Moon: Power Ripens Fruit - Become Victory of Prophecy

**Dali** *22/10*

Yellow Lunar Human

Kin: 132

Sun 25/4

**Seli** *23/10*

☾♎7.02pm

Red Electric Skywalker

Kin: 133

Mon 26/4

**Gamma** *24/10*

○3.31pm

White Self-Existing Wizard

Kin: 134

Tue 27/4

**Kali** *25/10*

♇℞6am

☾♏6.26pm

Blue Overtone Eagle

Kin: 135

Wed 28/4

# MOON OF MANIFESTATION

Alpha 26/10

Yellow Rhythmic Warrior

Kin: 136

Thu 29/4

1 Eb

☾♐6.38pm

Limi 27/10

Red Resonant Earth

Kin: 137

Fri 30/4 SAMHAIN

☿♉12.12pm

Silio 28/10

White Galactic Mirror

Kin: 138

Sat 1/5

Week 1/13

# 13 MOON SYNCHRONOMETER - 11TH MOON OF BLUE LUNAR STORM YEAR

| DALI SUNDAY | SELI MONDAY | GAMMA TUESDAY | KALI WEDNESDAY | ALPHA THURSDAY | LIMI FRIDAY | SILIO SATURDAY |
|---|---|---|---|---|---|---|
| 139 MAY 2 BLUE SOLAR STORM **1** | 140 MAY 3 YELLOW PLANETARY SUN **2** | 141 MAY 4 RED SPECTRAL DRAGON **3** | 142 MAY 5 WHITE CRYSTAL WIND **4** | 143 MAY 6 BLUE COSMIC NIGHT **5** | 144 MAY 7 YELLOW MAGNETIC SEED **6** | 145 MAY 8 RED LUNAR SERPENT **7** |
| 146 MAY 9 WHITE ELECTRIC WORLDBRIDGER **8** | 147 MAY 10 BLUE SELF-EXISTING HAND **9** | 148 MAY 11 YELLOW OVERTONE STAR **10** | 149 MAY 12 RED RHYTMIC MOON **11** | 150 MAY 13 WHITE RESONANT DOG **12** | 151 MAY 14 BLUE GALACTIC MONKEY **13** | 152 MAY 15 YELLOW SOLAR HUMAN **14** |
| 153 MAY 16 RED PLANETARY SKYWALKER **15** | 154 MAY 17 WHITE SPECTRAL WIZARD **16** | 155 MAY 18 BLUE CRYSTAL EAGLE **17** | 156 MAY 19 YELLOW COSMIC WARRIOR **18** | 157 MAY 20 RED MAGNETIC EARTH **19** | 158 MAY 21 WHITE LUNAR MIRROR **20** | 159 MAY 22 BLUE ELECTRIC STORM **21** |
| 160 MAY 23 YELLOW SELF-EXISTING SUN **22** | 161 MAY 24 RED OVERTONE DRAGON **23** | 162 MAY 25 WHITE RHYTMIC WIND **24** | 163 MAY 26 BLUE RESONANT NIGHT **25** | 164 MAY 27 YELLOW GALACTIC SEED **26** | 165 MAY 28 RED SOLAR SERPENT **27** | 166 MAY 29 WHITE PLANETARY WORLDBRIDGER **28** |

SPECTRAL SERPENT MOON — How do I Release & Let Go?

TRANSFORMATION

Heidi Holland
IG thou.art.revolution

# RED WEEK INITIATE

Red Week One - Spectral Serpent Moon: Knowledge Initiates View - Claim Power of Prophecy

Dali 1/11

☾♑9.16pm

Blue Solar Storm

Kin: 139

(15) *'In order to see into darkness'*

Sun 2/5

Seli 2/11

Yellow Planetary Sun

Kin: 140

Mon 3/5

Gamma 3/11

♀♉7.56pm

Red Spectral Dragon

Kin: 141

Tue 4/5

Kali 4/11

☾♒3.14am

White Crystal Wind

Kin: 142

Wed 5/5

# MOON OF LIBERATION

Alpha 5/11

Blue Cosmic Night

Kin: 143

Thu 6/5

YELLOW SEED WAVESPELL 4

Power of Flowering

☾♓12.25pm

Limi 6/11

Yellow Magnetic Seed

Kin: 144

Fri 7/5

Silio 7/11

Red Lunar Serpent

Kin: 145

Sat 8/5

Week 2/13

# WHITE WEEK
# REFINE

White Week Two - Spectral Serpent Moon: Humility Refines Meditation - Maintain Power of Prophecy

Dali 8/11

☾♈ 11.59pm

White Electric World-Bridger

Kin: 146

Sun 9/5

Seli 9/11

Blue Self-Existing Hand

Kin: 147

MOTHERS DAY

Mon 10/5

Gamma 10/11

Yellow Overtone Star

Kin: 148

Tue 11/5

Kali 11/11

● 6.59am

☾♉ 12.48pm

Red Rhythmic Moon

Kin: 149

Wed 12/5

# MOON OF LIBERATION

1 Chicchan

Alpha 12/11

White Resonant Dog

Thu 13/5

Limi 13/11

Blue Galactic Monkey

Fri 14/5

☾♊1.44am
☉♉5.55am

Silio 14/11

Yellow Solar Human

Sat 15/5

Week 3/13

Blue Week Three - Spectral Serpent Moon: Patience Transforms Conduct - Maintain Power of Prophecy

Dali 15/11

Red Planetary Skywalker

Kin: 153

Sun 16/5

Seli 16/11

☾♋1.23pm

White Spectral Wizard

Kin: 154

Mon 17/5

Gamma 17/11

Blue Crystal Eagle

Kin: 155

Tue 18/5

Kali 18/11

☾♌10.18pm

Yellow Cosmic Warrior

Kin: 156

Wed 19/5

# MOON OF LIBERATION

RED EARTH WAVESPELL 17
Power of Navigation

Alpha 19/11

Red Magnetic Earth

YELLOW SOUTHERN CASTLE OF GIVING (Kins 157-208/52-days)
Court of Intelligence: Ripen Sun

Thu 20/5

Limi 20/11

White Lunar Mirror

Fri 21/5

☾♍3.37am

Silio 21/11

Blue Electric Storm

Sat 22/5

*(16) 'Touching a music of the future'*

Week 4/13

# YELLOW WEEK
# RIPEN

Yellow Week Four - Spectral Serpent Moon: Power Ripens Fruit - Become Victory of Prophecy

Dali 22/11

♄℞ 9.03pm

Yellow Self-Existing Sun

Kin: 160

BLUE GALACTIC SPECTRUM (Kins 55-119/65-days)
Eagle Season of Vision

Sun 23/5

Seli 23/11

☾♎ 5.34am

Red Overtone Dragon

Kin: 161

Mon 24/5

Gamma 24/11

White Rhythmic Wind

Kin: 162

Tue 25/5

Kali 25/11

1 Etznab
☾♏ 5.25am
☿♊ 3.01pm
○ 3.01pm
☍ Lunar Eclipse

Blue Resonant Night

Kin: 163

Wed 26/5

# MOON OF LIBERATION

Alpha 26/11

Yellow Galactic Seed

Thu 27/5

☾♐4.59am

Limi 27/11

Red Solar Serpent

Fri 28/5

♀♊6.31am

Silio 28/11

White Planetary World-Bridger

Sat 29/5

Week 5/13

# 13 MOON SYNCHRONOMETER - 12TH MOON OF BLUE LUNAR STORM YEAR

| DALI SUNDAY | SELI MONDAY | GAMMA TUESDAY | KALI WEDNESDAY | ALPHA THURSDAY | LIMI FRIDAY | SILIO SATURDAY |
|---|---|---|---|---|---|---|
| 167 MAY 30 BLUE SPECTRAL HAND **1** | 168 MAY 31 YELLOW CRYSTAL STAR **2** | 169 JUN 1 RED COSMIC MOON **3** | 170 JUN 2 WHITE MAGNETIC DOG **4** | 171 JUN 3 BLUE LUNAR MONKEY **5** | 172 JUN 4 YELLOW ELECTRIC HUMAN **6** | 173 JUN 5 RED SELF-EXISTING SKYWALKER **7** |
| 174 JUN 6 WHITE OVERTONE WIZARD **8** | 175 JUN 7 BLUE RHYTMIC EAGLE **9** | 176 JUN 8 YELLOW RESONANT WARRIOR **10** | 177 JUN 9 RED GALACTIC EARTH **11** | 178 JUN 10 WHITE SOLAR MIRROR **12** | 179 JUN 11 BLUE PLANETARY STORM **13** | 180 JUN 12 YELLOW SPECTRAL SUN **14** |
| 181 JUN 13 RED CRYSTAL DRAGON **15** | 182 JUN 14 WHITE COSMIC WIND **16** | 183 JUN 15 BLUE MAGNETIC NIGHT **17** | 184 JUN 16 YELLOW LUNAR SEED **18** | 185 JUN 17 RED ELECTRIC SERPENT **19** | 186 JUN 18 WHITE SELF-EXISTING WORLDBRIDGER **20** | 187 JUN 19 BLUE OVERTONE HAND **21** |
| 188 JUN 20 YELLOW RHYTMIC STAR **22** | 189 JUN 21 RED RESONANT MOON **23** | 190 JUN 22 WHITE GALACTIC DOG **24** | 191 JUN 23 BLUE SOLAR MONKEY **25** | 192 JUN 24 YELLOW PLANETARY HUMAN **26** | 193 JUN 25 RED SPECTRAL SKYWALKER **27** | 194 JUN 26 WHITE CRYSTAL WIZARD **28** |

**CRYSTAL RABBIT MOON** — How can I Dedicate myself to all that lives?

INNER BLOOM Anakayla Stevenson-Ambroz ♥
www.solarrhythm.com

## RED WEEK
# INITIATE

Red Week One - Crystal Rabbit Moon: Knowledge Initiates View - Claim Power of Prophecy

Dali 1/12

☾♑6.09am
☿℞10.33am

Blue Spectral Hand

Sun 30/5

Seli 2/12

Yellow Crystal Star

Mon 31/5

Gamma 3/12

☾♒10.29am

Red Cosmic Moon

Tue 1/6

Kali 4/12

WHITE DOG WAVESPELL 10
Power of Heart

♂♋1.22pm

White Magnetic Dog

Wed 2/6

# MOON OF COOPERATION

☿℞♉9.04am
☽♓6.37pm

Alpha 5/12

Blue Lunar Monkey

Kin: 171

Thu 3/6

Limi 6/12

Yellow Electric Human

Kin: 172

Fri 4/6

☽♈5.17am

Silio 7/12

Red Self-Existing Skywalker

Kin: 173

Sat 5/6

Week 6/13

# WHITE WEEK
# REFINE

White Week Two - Crystal Rabbit Moon: Humility Refines Meditation - Maintain Power of Prophecy

**Dali** 8/12

White Overtone Wizard

Kin: 174

Sun 6/6

**Seli** 9/12

Blue Rhythmic Eagle

Kin: 175

Mon 7/6

**Gamma** 10/12

1 Chuen

☾♉6.53pm

Yellow Resonant Warrior

Kin: 176

Tue 8/6

**Kali** 11/12

Red Galactic Earth

Kin: 177

Wed 9/6

# MOON OF COOPERATION

●10.52pm
☌Annular Solar Eclipse

Alpha 12/12

White Solar Mirror

Kin: 178

Thu 10/6

☾♊7.40am

Limi 13/12

Blue Planetary Storm

Kin: 179

Fri 11/6

*(17) 'With the song and the rhythym'*

Silio 14/12

Yellow Spectral Sun

Kin: 180

Sat 12/6

Week 7/13

# BLUE WEEK TRANSFORM

Blue Week Three - Crystal Rabbit Moon: Patience Transforms Conduct - Maintain Power of Prophecy

**Dali** 15/12

☾♋7.02pm

Red Crystal Dragon

Kin: 181

Sun 13/6

**Seli** 16/12

White Cosmic Wind

Kin: 182

Mon 14/6

**Gamma** 17/12

BLUE NIGHT WAVESPELL 3

Power of Abundance

☉♊12.31pm

Blue Magnetic Night

Kin: 183

Tue 15/6

**Kali** 18/12

☾♌4.12am

Yellow Lunar Seed

Kin: 184

Wed 16/6

# MOON OF COOPERATION

Alpha 19/12

Red Electric Serpent

Kin: 185

RED GALACTIC SPECTRUM (Kins 185-249/65-days)
Serpent Season of Life Force

Thu 17/6

☾♍10.37am

Limi 20/12

White Self-Existing World-Bridger

Kin: 186

Fri 18/6

Silio 21/12

Blue Overtone Hand

Kin: 187

Sat 19/6

Week 8/13

# YELLOW WEEK
# RIPEN

Yellow Week Four - Crystal Rabbit Moon: Power Ripens Fruit - Become Victory of Prophecy

Dali 22/12

☽♎2.13pm

Yellow Rhythmic Star

Kin: 188

Sun 20/6

Seli 23/12

1 Kan

♃℞2.50am

Red Resonant Moon

Kin: 189

SOLSTICE

Mon 21/6

Gamma 24/12

☽♏3.30pm

♀♋8.52pm

White Galactic Dog

Kin: 190

Tue 22/6

Kali 25/12

☿D10.02am

♃℞D10.02am

Blue Solar Monkey

Kin: 191

Wed 23/6

# MOON OF COOPERATION

☾♐3.41pm

Alpha 26/12

Yellow Planetary Human

Kin: 192

Thu 24/6

○6.39am

Limi 27/12

Red Spectral Skywalker

Kin: 193

Fri 25/6

♆℞3.26am

☾♑4.25pm

Silio 28/12

White Crystal Wizard

Kin: 194

Sat 26/6

Week 9/13

# 13 MOON SYNCHRONOMETER - 13TH MOON OF BLUE LUNAR STORM YEAR

| DALI SUNDAY | SELI MONDAY | GAMMA TUESDAY | KALI WEDNESDAY | ALPHA THURSDAY | LIMI FRIDAY | SILIO SATURDAY |
|---|---|---|---|---|---|---|
| 195 JUN 27 BLUE COSMIC EAGLE 1 | 196 JUN 28 YELLOW MAGNETIC WARRIOR 2 | 197 JUN 29 RED LUNAR EARTH 3 | 198 JUN 30 WHITE ELECTRIC MIRROR 4 | 199 JUL 1 BLUE SELF-EXISTING STORM 5 | 200 JUL 2 YELLOW OVERTONE SUN 6 | 201 JUL 3 RED RHYTMIC DRAGON 7 |
| 202 JUL 4 WHITE RESONANT WIND 8 | 203 JUL 5 BLUE GALACTIC NIGHT 9 | 204 JUL 6 YELLOW SOLAR SEED 10 | 205 JUL 7 RED PLANETARY SERPENT 11 | 206 JUL 8 WHITE SPECTRAL WORLDBRIDGER 12 | 207 JUL 9 BLUE CRYSTAL HAND 13 | 208 JUL 10 YELLOW COSMIC STAR ● 14 |
| 209 JUL 11 RED MAGNETIC MOON 15 | 210 JUL 12 WHITE LUNAR DOG 16 | 211 JUL 13 BLUE ELECTRIC MONKEY 17 | 212 JUL 14 YELLOW SELF-EXISTING HUMAN 18 | 213 JUL 15 RED OVERTONE SKYWALKER 19 | 214 JUL 16 WHITE RHYTMIC WIZARD 20 | 215 JUL 17 BLUE RESONANT EAGLE 21 |
| 216 JUL 18 YELLOW GALACTIC WARRIOR 22 | 217 JUL 19 RED SOLAR EARTH 23 | 218 JUL 20 WHITE PLANETARY MIRROR 24 | 219 JUL 21 BLUE SPECTRAL STORM 25 | 220 JUL 22 YELLOW CRYSTAL SUN 26 | 221 JUL 23 RED COSMIC DRAGON 27 | 222 JUL 24 WHITE MAGNETIC WIND ○ 28 |

COSMIC TURTLE MOON

How can I Extend my Love & Joy?

SERENE IN THE SEA OF MYSTERY Hope Fiorenza
www.facebook.com/hoperebornart/

# RED WEEK INITIATE

Red Week One - Cosmic Turtle Moon: Knowledge Initiates View - Claim Power of Prophecy

Dali 1/13

Blue Cosmic Eagle

Kin: 195

Sun 27/6

Seli 2/13

YELLOW WARRIOR WAVESPELL 16

Power of Intelligence

☾♒7.30pm

Yellow Magnetic Warrior

Kin: 196

Mon 28/6

Gamma 3/13

Red Lunar Earth

Kin: 197

Tue 29/6

Kali 4/13

White Electric Mirror

Kin: 198

Wed 30/6

# MOON OF PRESENCE

☾♓2.13am

Alpha 5/13

Blue Self-Existing Storm

Kin: 199

Thu 1/7 (18) *'Located in the correct place where the food of divination is found'*

Limi 6/13

Yellow Overtone Sun

Kin: 200

Fri 2/7

☾♈12.44pm

Silio 7/13

Red Rhythmic Dragon

Kin: 201

Sat 3/7

Week 10/13

# WHITE WEEK
# REFINE

White Week Two - Cosmic Turtle Moon: Humility Refines Meditation - Maintain Power of Prophecy

Dali 8/13

1 Caban

White Resonant Wind

Kin: 202

Sun 4/7

Seli 9/13

Blue Galactic Night

Kin: 203

Mon 5/7

Gamma 10/13

☾♉1.30am

Yellow Solar Seed

Kin: 204

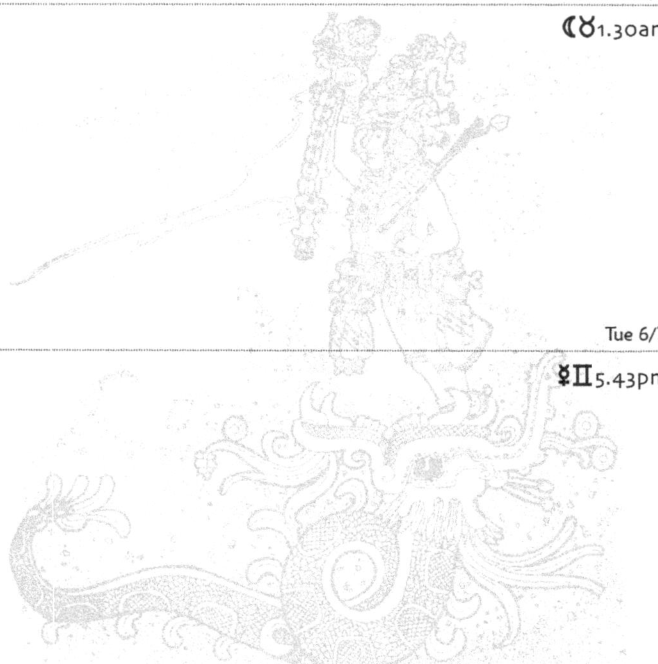

Tue 6/7

Kali 11/13

☿♊5.43pm

Red Planetary Serpent

Kin: 205

Wed 7/7

# MOON OF PRESENCE

☾♊ 2.12pm

Alpha 12/13

White Spectral World-Bridger

Kin: 206

Thu 8/7

Limi 13/13

Blue Crystal Hand

Kin: 207

Fri 9/7

● 1.16pm

Silio 14/13

Yellow Cosmic Star

Kin: 208

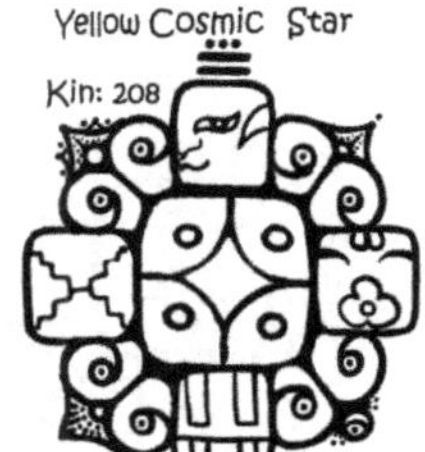

Sat 10/7 MONKEY GENESIS COMPLETE

Blue Week Three - Cosmic Turtle Moon: Patience Transforms Conduct - Maintain Power of Prophecy

Dali 15/13

RED MOON WAVESPELL 9
Power of Universal Water

Red Magnetic Moon

Kin: 209

MOON GENESIS - Power of Magical Flight (Kins 209-260/52-days)
GREEN CENTRAL CASTLE OF ENCHANTMENT (Kins 209-260/52-days)
Court of th Matrix : Synchronise Human

Sun 11/7

Seli 16/13

White Lunar Dog

Kin: 210

Mon 12/7

Gamma 17/13

☾♌9.44am

Blue Electric Monkey

Kin: 211

Tue 13/7

Kali 18/13

Yellow Self-Existing Human

Kin: 212

Wed 14/7

# MOON OF PRESENCE

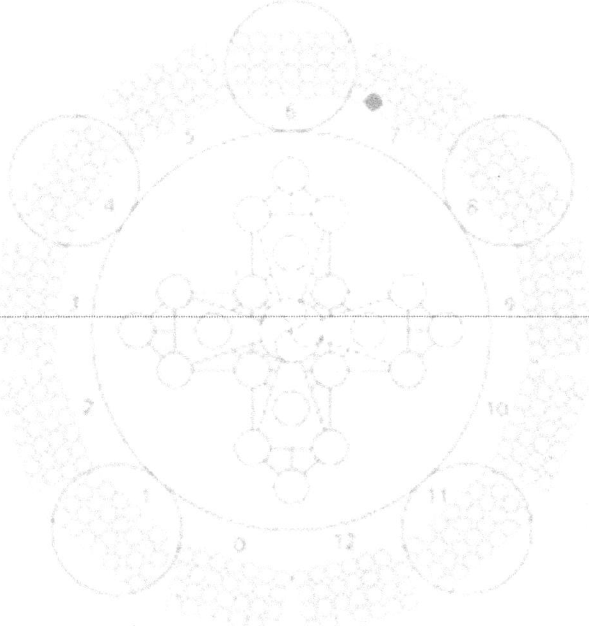

☾♍4.09pm

Alpha 19/13

Red Overtone Skywalker

Kin: 213

Thu 15/7

⚷℞4.15am
☉♋11.24pm

Limi 20/13

White Rhythmic Wizard

Kin: 214

Fri 16/7

1 Oc
♀♌3.56pm
☾♎8.37pm

Silio 21/13

Blue Resonant Eagle

Kin: 215

Sat 17/7

Week 12/13

# YELLOW WEEK
# RIPEN

Yellow Week Four - Cosmic Turtle Moon: Power Ripens Fruit - Become Victory of Prophecy

**Dali** *22/13*

Yellow Galactic Warrior

Kin: 216

Sun 18/7

**Seli** *23/13*

☾♏ 11.24pm

Red Solar Earth

Kin: 217

Mon 19/7

**Gamma** *24/13*

White Planetary Mirror

Kin: 218

Tue 20/7

**Kali** *25/13*

♂♌ 12.25am

Blue Spectral Storm

Kin: 219

*(Uayeb) 'All that is needed in order to obtain the precious stone'* Wed 21/7

○ ○ ○

# MOON OF PRESENCE

☾♐1am

Alpha 26/13

Yellow Crystal Sun

Kin: 220

Thu 22/7

Limi 27/13

Red Cosmic Dragon

Kin: 221

Fri 23/7

Silio 28/13

WHITE WIND WAVESPELL 2

Power of Spirit

☾♑2.28am

○2.37pm

White Magnetic Wind

Kin: 222

Sat 24/7

Week 13/13

# DAY OUT OF TIME

Blue Lunar Night

☿♋6.12pm

Kin: 223

International Water Day

Mon 25/7

The Day Out Of Time (DOOT) is the 365th day of the Year or Solar Spin. It is acknowledged as a day for Celebration and Forgiveness, in Dedication to Healing of the Planetary Waters!

There hae been an increasing number of DOOT Events celebrated worldwide for the past 29 years. To find an event near you, or even to stage one and let others know, refer to https://lawoftime.org/day-out-of-time

## Let's look 2 mOOns ahead!

# mOOns 1 & 2 of YELLOW ELECTRIC SEED year

| DALI MONDAY | SELI TUESDAY | GAMMA WEDNESDAY | KALI THURSDAY | ALPHA FRIDAY | LIMI SATURDAY | SILIO SUNDAY |
|---|---|---|---|---|---|---|
| 224 JUL 26 YELLOW ELECTRIC SEED **1** | 225 JUL 27 RED SELF-EXISTING SERPENT **2** | 226 JUL 28 WHITE OVERTONE WORLDBRIDGER **3** | 227 JUL 29 BLUE RHYTHMIC HAND **4** | 228 JUL 30 YELLOW RESONANT STAR **5** | 229 JUL 31 RED GALACTIC MOON **6** | 230 AUG 1 WHITE SOLAR DOG **7** |
| 231 AUG 2 BLUE PLANETARY MONKEY **8** | 232 AUG 3 YELLOW SPECTRAL HUMAN **9** | 233 AUG 4 RED CRYSTAL SKYWALKER **10** | 234 AUG 5 WHITE COSMIC WIZARD **11** | 235 AUG 6 BLUE MAGNETIC EAGLE **12** | 236 AUG 7 YELLOW LUNAR WARRIOR **13** | 237 AUG 8 RED ELECTRIC EARTH ● **14** |
| 238 AUG 9 WHITE SELF-EXISTING MIRROR **15** | 239 AUG 10 BLUE OVERTONE STORM **16** | 240 AUG 11 YELLOW RHYTHMIC SUN **17** | 241 AUG 12 RED RESONANT DRAGON **18** | 242 AUG 13 WHITE GALACTIC WIND **19** | 243 AUG 14 BLUE SOLAR NIGHT **20** | 244 AUG 15 YELLOW PLANETARY SEED **21** |
| 245 AUG 16 RED SPECTRAL SERPENT **22** | 246 AUG 17 WHITE CRYSTAL WORLDBRIDGER **23** | 247 AUG 18 BLUE COSMIC HAND **24** | 248 AUG 19 YELLOW MAGNETIC STAR **25** | 249 AUG 20 RED LUNAR MOON **26** | 250 AUG 21 WHITE ELECTRIC DOG **27** | 251 AUG 22 BLUE SELF-EXISTING MONKEY ○ **28** |

MAGNETIC BAT MOON ●

What Is My Purpose?

| DALI MONDAY | SELI TUESDAY | GAMMA WEDNESDAY | KALI THURSDAY | ALPHA FRIDAY | LIMI SATURDAY | SILIO SUNDAY |
|---|---|---|---|---|---|---|
| 252 AUG 23 YELLOW OVERTONE HUMAN **1** | 253 AUG 24 RED RHYTHMIC SKYWALKER **2** | 254 AUG 25 WHITE RESONANT WIZARD **3** | 255 AUG 26 BLUE GALACTIC EAGLE **4** | 256 AUG 27 YELLOW SOLAR WARRIOR **5** | 257 AUG 28 RED PLANETARY EARTH **6** | 258 AUG 29 WHITE SPECTRAL MIRROR **7** |
| 259 AUG 30 BLUE CRYSTAL STORM **8** | 260 AUG 31 YELLOW COSMIC SUN **9** | 1 SEP 1 RED MAGNETIC DRAGON **10** | 2 SEP 2 WHITE LUNAR WIND **11** | 3 SEP 3 BLUE ELECTRIC NIGHT **12** | 4 SEP 4 YELLOW SELF-EXISTING SEED **13** | 5 SEP 5 RED OVERTONE SERPENT **14** |
| 6 SEP 6 WHITE RHYTHMIC WORLDBRIDGER **15** | 7 SEP 7 BLUE RESONANT HAND ● **16** | 8 SEP 8 YELLOW GALACTIC STAR **17** | 9 SEP 9 RED SOLAR MOON **18** | 10 SEP 10 WHITE PLANETARY DOG **19** | 11 SEP 11 BLUE SPECTRAL MONKEY **20** | 12 SEP 12 YELLOW CRYSTAL HUMAN **21** |
| 13 SEP 13 RED COSMIC SKYWALKER **22** | 14 SEP 14 WHITE MAGNETIC WIZARD **23** | 15 SEP 15 BLUE LUNAR EAGLE **24** | 16 SEP 16 YELLOW ELECTRIC WARRIOR **25** | 17 SEP 17 RED SELF-EXISTING EARTH **26** | 18 SEP 18 WHITE OVERTONE MIRROR **27** | 19 SEP 19 BLUE RHYTHMIC STORM **28** |

LUNAR SCORPION MOON ●●

What Is My Challenge?

# GALACTIC COSMOLOGY

The 20 tribes divide into 10 pairs of planetary partners according to the 10 planetary orbits of Kinich Ahau (the Sun), which makes up our Solar System. There are 5 inner and 5 outer planets with maintain the orbit of the galactic breath of Kinich Ahau - the galactic-in, and the solar-out breaths of the circulation of time. Through co-operation the 20 tribes maintain the power of the galactic-solar circular breath as Radial Kin.

## OUTER FIVE PLANETS

Galactic Terminal

**PLUTO ♇ 10th orbit:**
**In:** **SUN** generates galactic matrix as universal fire. **Alpha**
**Out:** **STORM** climaxes solar matrix as self-generation. **Omega**

**Neptune ♆ 9th orbit:**
**In:** **DRAGON** transmits galactic input as birth.
**Out:** **MIRROR** protects solar matrix as endlessness.

Uranus Transfer

**URANUS ♅ 8th orbit:**
**In:** **WIND** energises galactic input as spirit.
**Out:** **EARTH** energises solar matrix as navigation.

**SATURN ♄ 7th orbit:**
**In:** **Night** protects galactic matrix as abundance.
**Out:** **Warrior** transmits solar output as intelligence.

Midway Transfer

**JUPITER ♃ 6th orbit:**
**In:** **SEED** climaxes galactic input as flowering.
**Out:** **EAGLE** generates solar output as vision.

## INNER FIVE PLANETS (PLACE OF TIME WARS AT -3187 YEARS)

**MALDEK** (NOW THE ASTEROID BELT) **5th orbit:**
**In:** **SERPENT** generates galactic store as life force.
**Out:** **WIZARD** climaxes solar output as timelessness.

Earth Transfer

**MARS ♂ 4th orbit:**
**In:** **WORLDBRIDGER** transmits galactic store as death.
**Out:** **SKYWALKER** protects solar output as space.

**EARTH ⊕3rd orbit:**
**In:** **HAND** energises galactic store as accomplishment.
**Out:** **HUMAN** energises solar process as free will.

Solar Terminal

**VENUS ♀ 2nd orbit:**
**In:** **STAR** protects galactic store as elegance.
**Out:** **MONKEY** transmits solar process as magic.

**MERCURY ☿ 1st orbit:**
**In:** **MOON** climaxes galactic process as universal water. **Omega**
**Out:** **DOG** generates solar process as heart. **Alpha**

At the beginning of the experiment of our Solar System, the 10 tribes enjoyed the radial evolution of attempting to create the harmony that unifes in order to transcend life and death. The pivot of this radial evolution was directly between Jupiter and Maldek, where the time wars began - free will misconceptions and conflicts orginating at the Midway Transfer between two sets of clans. The 1st wave reduced Maldek to an orbiting set of Asteroids, the 2nd eliminated the experiment on Mars. Now all hope for the star system Kinich Ahau is placed in the 3rd planet, Earth. As long as Earth still holds its orbit, the time tunnel between the 3rd and 8th planets can be completed, which can allow the Kinich Ahau system to sound the galactic 5th chord of unifying harmony. After the disasters of Maldek and Mars, the 20 planetary partners regroup as the 4 Root Races, red, white, blue, yellow, creating the Rainbow Nation. Earth is targeted to create galactic-solar harmony through the seeding and evolving of this Rainbow Nation.

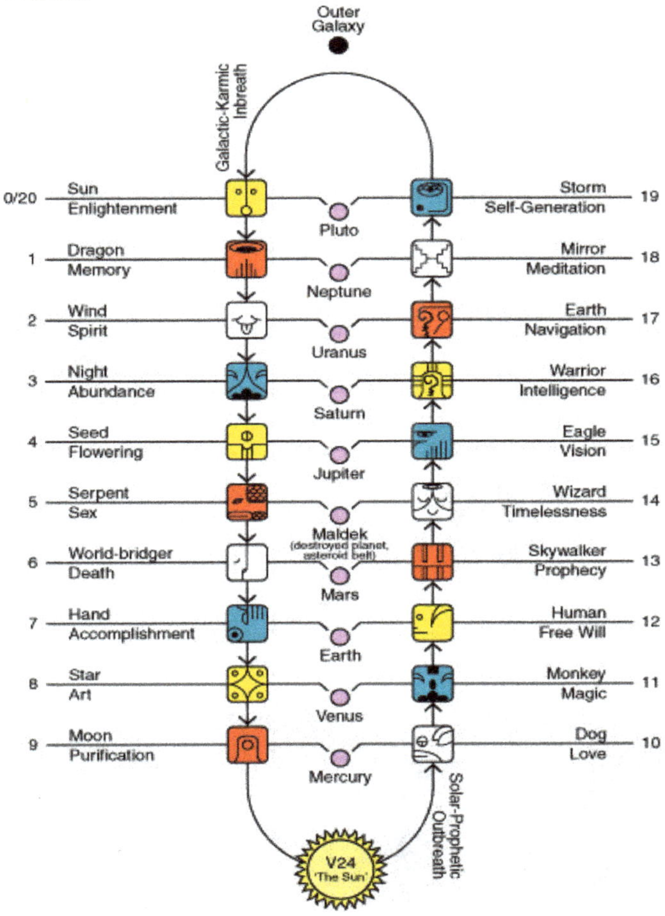

# PLANETS

Courtesy of Ellias Lonsdale
& Mark Borax
www.stargenesiswisdom.com
www.markborax.com

### Personal Planets

☉ **SUN,** rules Leo - *The Sun takes approximately 365 days to travel through the Zodiac, and spends 30 days in each sign.*
Planet of Self (Central Planet). Integrate, will, energy and power, stamina. Central flame of identity. Cosmic universal center of greater selfhood, bringing all-that-is into earthly expression.

☽ **MOON**, rules Cancer - *Swiftest of all celestial bodies. Travels thru the Zodiac in approx 28 days, spends around 2 ¼ days in each sign.*
Planet Of Needs And Feelings. React, reflect, change (rhythmical), fluctuation. Emotional realm, dreaming. Least consciousness-oriented planet. Sentiment, body, energy, rather than intuition. Doesn't know how to see, it feels things. Your relationship to your environment, to public. Moon = nothing happens to you, everything happens thru you.

☿ **MERCURY**, rules Gemini & Virgo – *Mercury's revolution takes about 88 days. Due to its frequent retrograde motion it spends a variable amount of time each sign.*
Planet of Mind. Communicate, speech, thought, short journeys, inquiry. Aliveness catalyst, traveling juggler, world-responder. One planet designated to circulate freely among all & bring news from the front. Principle of right interaction & full exchange.

♀ **VENUS**, rules Taurus & Libra - *variable cycle, takes approx 225 days to travel through the Zodiac, with around18¾ days in each sign.*
Planet Of Pleasure And Luxury. Harmonise, liking (enjoy, link), evaluation, attraction, joining together. Intact inner voice that will see us through. Emphasizes what's meant to happen in an ideal way. Interior private treasure wholeheartedly kept intact for time of full opening. Where you sit in self, beingness. Asks individual to choose between self-serving & life-giving elements of each sign. Likes to finish things well. The finisher.

♂ **MARS**, rules Aries & Scorpio - *This quite small planet travels through the Zodiac in 1 year & 220 days. Usually spending about 8 weeks in each sign, although at certain stages of his cycle, can remain in the same sign for 5 or 6 months.*
Planet Of Physical Energy. Action, assertion, initiation, division. Champion of radical self-overcoming. Putting all drive in a singular direction. Wants to claim individual freedom.

## *Transpersonal Planets*

♃ **JUPITER**, rules Sagittarius & Pisces - *first slow-moving planet, biggest of the solar system, takes 11 years & 11 moons to travel through the Zodiac, spending approx a year per sign.*
Planet Of Expansion. Generalisation and abstraction, truth seeking, benevolence. Beacon of future, harbinger of all good, instrumenter of greater design into tangible form. Leads us from obscurity to the truth beyond memory, the Big Picture.

♄ **SATURN**, rules Capricorn & Aquarius - *takes about 29 years to travel through the Zodiac, and spends around 2½ years in each sign.*
Planet of Time, Discipline, Responsibilities and Hard Work. Control, limitation, discipline, responsibility, rejection, must do. Calls for self-confrontation. Directs all planets. Destiny clarifier. Core persistence.

## *Transcendent Planets*

♅ **URANUS**, rules Aquarius - *takes some 84 years to travel through the Zodiac, and spends about 7 years in each sign.*
Planet Of Revolution. Invention, inspiration, freedom, awaken. The subtle magician-wizard within. Planetary initiation into expanded states of being and consciousness. Alchemical mix. Advanced personal consciousness, where you as an individual stretch beyond all known boundaries and all other parts of you.

♆ **NEPTUNE**, rules Pisces - *takes approx 168 years to travel through the Zodiac and spends roughly 14 years in each sign.*
Planet Of Transcendence. Refinement, transcendence, mystery, surrender, dissolution. What we all most have in common. Stretches all boundaries to make way for galactic forces to take place in Earth evolution. Collective consciousness. The primary world dream being dreamed during a given point in world history and awareness.

♇⯓ **PLUTO**, rules Scorpio - *takes approx 254 years to travel through the Zodiac, and can remain in a sign for 12 to 30 years.*
Planet Of Transformation. Regenerate, eliminate, purge, redeem. Master of disguises, revealer of essences. Dancing out a code inscribing what is missing in human experience. Pulling in from all greater worlds a response to the crying human need.

⚷ **ALPHA OMEGA** (Chiron) - *takes around 51 years to travel through the zodiac, spending approx 4¼ years in each sign.*
Wounded Healer, Great Teacher. To bring out the fullest potential, to teach, to unlock, to find what is essential, to reconcile opposites (shaman), to heal holistically. Wisdom, patience and the capacity to relieve other people's sufferings. Streamlines the way through. Call station to assist further evolution of the planet. Quickens, vitalises.

☊ **NORTH NODE** - *The Moon's North Node takes about 18 years to travel through the Zodiac and takes roughly 1½ years in each sign.* Indicates direction, area and manner in which the collective destiny is sought.

# ASTROLOGICAL SIGNS

♈ **Aries the Ram** - Fire, Cardinal, 'I am' - birth, beginning, incentive, activate, bold, optimistic, courageous, direct, raw, enthusiastic, dynamic, fast, impulsive, adventurous, naive, Strong willed, Do it! Initiate action. Going forward, emergence into the World. Male sex drive. **Ruled by Mars**

♉ **Taurus the Bull, Taura the Cow** - Earth, Fixed, 'I have' - earth-loving, loyal, patient, focused, stable, realistic, hard-working, constructive, tenacious. Stamina & building, rewards. Love of physical pleasures & material goods, delicious excess. Tactile enjoying a tender, sensual, touch **Ruled by Venus**

♊ **Gemini the Twins** - Air, Mutable, 'I think' - expressive, lively, adaptable, quick-witted, humorous, sociable, curious, whimsical, independent, flexible, imaginative, scattered, moody, inquisitive, fragile, ironical or changeable. Language and social communications, family links. **Ruled by Mercury**

♋ **Cancer the Crab** - Water, Cardinal, 'I feel' - emotional, sentimental, sensitive, faithful, protective, generous, romantic, nostalgic, tender, poetic-minded, motherly, dreamy, evasive, passive, dependent, moody, lazy, touchy, Fertility and childbearing. Parenthood and nurturance. **Ruled by Moon**

♌ **Leo the Lion** - Fire, Fixed, 'I love' - creative, warm hearted, passionate, dramatic, proud, determined, strong-willed, generous, ambitious, heroic, confident, seductive, happy, daring, majestic, honest, magnanimous, charismatic, responsible, noble but also domineering, self-centred. **Ruled by Sun**

♍ **Virgo the Virgin** - Earth, Mutable, 'I serve' - attentive to detail & numbers, analytical, serious, competent, sensible, modest, logical, tidy, well-organized, clean, hard-working, honest, faithful, reserved, helpful, perfectionist, narrow-minded. Relationships of teamwork, co-operation and service. **Ruled by Mercury & Chiron**

♎ **Libra the Scales** - Air, Cardinal, 'We are' - sentimental, fair, charming, polite, refined, pacifist, distinguished, light-hearted, romantic, creative, well-groomed, calm, sweet, tolerant, elegant, sociable, seductive, aesthetic. Relationships of marriage & partnership, community. **Ruled by Venus & Ceres**

♏ **Scorpio the Scorpion** - Water, Fixed, 'We have' - secretive, powerful, domineering, resistant, intuitive, charismatic, magnetic, passionate, independent, untameable, possessive, sexual, intense, destructive, stubborn, complex. Death & renewal. Female sex drive. **Ruled by Pluto**

♐ **Sagittarius the Archer** - Fire, Mutable, 'We think' - charismatic, energetic, likeable, benevolent, jovial, optimising, amusing, bold, extroverted, straight-forward, demonstrative, independent, adventurous, exuberant, freedom-loving, travel, expansion, teaching/learning. Spiritual Life, abundance. **Ruled by Jupiter**

♑ **Capricorn the Goat** - Earth, Cardinal, 'We achieve' - serious, disciplined, patient, focused, ambitious, indomitable, cautious, provident, stern, wilful, hard-working, responsible, realistic, reserved, moralistic, quiet, reliable. slow or sceptical. Profession, attainment, maturity & silence. **Ruled by Saturn**

♒ **Aquarius the Water-bearer** - Air, Fixed, 'We love' - idealistic, altruistic, detached, independent, original, gifted, innovative, humanistic, friendly, self-confident, creative, charitable, elusive, tolerant, paradoxical, freedom-loving, utopian, eccentric. Change, Renewal through friendship. **Ruled by Uranus**

♓ **Pisces the Fish** - Water, Mutable, 'We serve' - emotional, sensitive, devoted, adaptable, compassionate, romantic, imaginative, flexible, fluid, intuitive, irrational, seductive, introverted, artistic, indecisive, confused, wavering, vulnerable, unpredictable and gullible, dissolving. Serenity & simplicity. **Ruled by Neptune**

# FURTHER IMMERSION

BOOKS AND SITES TO TAKE YOU DEEPER

## BOOKS

13 Moon & Dreamspell Workbook (Companion for this Day Book)
Available at **www.timewaves.org**

Mayan Factor, Earth Ascending, Time and the Technosphere
Arcturus Probe, Transformative Vision, Mandala
*JOSE ARGUELLES*

Cosmic History Chronicles - Volumes 1-7,
*JOSE ARGUELLES & STEPHANIE SOUTH*

The Uninscribed, 2012 Biography of a Time Traveller
Time, Synchronicity and Calendar Change
Accessing Your Multidimensional Self:
A Key to Cosmic History
*STEPHANIE SOUTH*

## BLOGS

www.timewaves.org
www.1320frequencyshift.wordpress.com
www.galacticwizard34.wordpress.com

## WEBSITES

www.1320sync.com
www.livingtimescience.com
www.timewaves.org
www.lawoftime.org
www.lawoftime.info
www.crest13.org
www.galacticspacebook.com
www.13moon.com
www.tomaash.net/13moons
www.13lunas.net
www.pan-holland.nl
www.mayankin.com
www.youtube.com/vasumizjikaa
www.19matrix.org
www.astrodreamadvisor.com/Mayan-Pages.html
www.astrosoundalchemy.bandcamp.com
www.galacticculture.wordpress.com
www.mayanmystic.com
www.tzolkin.krul.cc
www.stargazerli.com
www.sacredroad.org
www.starroot.com
www.zijnschool.nl

# IN GRATITUDE

Blessed be to Earth Mother and Sky Father, Papatuanuku and Ranginui for all that you gift all, each and every day. May we honour the abundance and share all that we receive.

In deep gratitude to the Ancient and Galactic Maya for having the foresight, wisdom and time-traveling capacities, to see this wisdom stored, in its purity in the Temples of Palenque. Released at this time in its pristine form for our future generations.

Profound thanks to Jose Arguelles/Valum Votan, Kin 11, for following the divine guidance of his mission, through synchronicity and dedication, to bring awareness of these Divine Codes to our planet.

Deep thanks to Lloydine Arguelles/Bolon Ik, Kin 22, for service in midwifing this work, in acknowledgement of your role.

Deep gratitude to Stephanie South/Red Queen, Kin 186, for taking up the baton. Thankyou for paving the way with clarity and love. In this time of co-creation, you are a pure inspiration with your humble, empowered dedication. Here for you sister!

Deep thanks to Tomaash, Kin 201, for the tech support updating these Day pages each year. Thankyou to Even DawnSong, Kin 25, for her artfull oracles that are included each year.
So appreciate you both for your ongoing support.

Thankyou to Elias Lonsdale and Rob Callahan for introducing me to worlds within worlds, within Star Genesis Astrology.

THANKYOU to my Big House Tribe for being there for me thru the creation of this years journal, for being open to exploring the experiment of 'Living the Harmonic Matrix'. Thankyou to Amrita for supporting this dreaming. Thankyou to our wider community.

Deep gratitude to all kin across the planet, dedicated to share this work.

Last but not least a huge THANKYOU to my Soul Family that gift a sense of Tribe, inspiring me to keep sharing on this Souls Path. You know who you are.

O YUM HUNAB KU EVA MAYA E MA HO!

# JOURNAL ORDERS & OFFERINGS

To continue to track the cycles of Time, order your new **13 Moon Synchronometer** for the coming Yellow Electric Seed year. Links are below.

To hear about ***Workshops, Events, Webinars, Wisdom Teachings, Mentoring*** *and* ***Video Transmissions***, **subscribe** to my **Website** or **Youtube Channel** below. Follow my **Facebook Page** or **join** the **Facebook Group** of the same name.

If it sings to your heart to become a ***Certified Dreamspell Teacher Trainings*** are now on offer. Once certified you will be supported to travel and teach.

And if any would like one of us to come to your area and share these teachings, invite and we will find someone close to you.

**Sacred Theatre Prayer-formance** is a wonderful way to activate a community into the New Time. We travel and share this in Communities, Festivals and Events worldwide. To participate in, or point to others that would like the same, feel free to invite us, we are a traveling Galactic ARTIVATION.

**One-on-One Sessions** are offered either in person or by Zoom through my **TimeWaves website**. Or simply **email me** for any of the above, or an introductory chat about Natural Time and how we can support each other and the Earth on this Planetary Mission

Lastly I give thanks to You, the Wisdom Seeker, for having the courage to consider a path less traveled. This is the fastest route to saving our planet, Changing our Time will Change our Minds, to patterns based in harmony & TIME IS ART!

**www.timewaves.org**
**IG: @lovevasumi**
**www.youtube.com/vasumizjikaa**
**Fb: Timewaves - the EVOLution rEVOLution (page and group)**

# DREAMSPELL WHEEL

Cut out this Wheel and align tribes and tones, to reveal wavespells, guides & earth families. It is easy to use and a most valuable tool in to track the Dreamspell. At every 1 dot tone the 2 tribes under will be the same - self-guided. Laminate each layer separately to give strength. In the end it should look like the wheel inside the white ring. Pierce the centre of each ring with a pin or wire to turn.

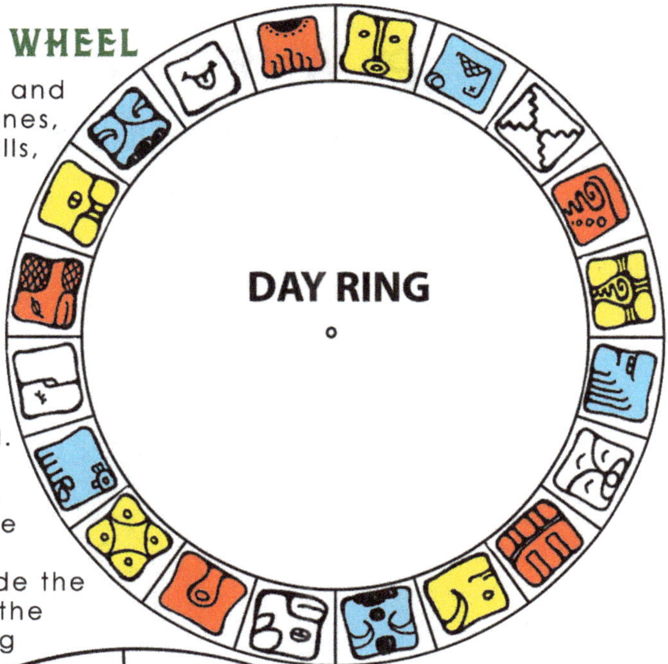

# PLANETARY KIN

A place for Contacts and Galactic Signatures

# DREAMSPELL WHEEL CONT.

The big wheel on this page doubles up with the tone wheel on the other page to be laminated together, to reveal the place on the Tzolkin, revealing GAP days and other synchronic alignments. The smallest wheel points out Earth Families. The Wavespell Ring reveals guides and castles. This is your own personal Magical Medicine Wheel. Enjoy this wondrous gift of Synchronic Time!

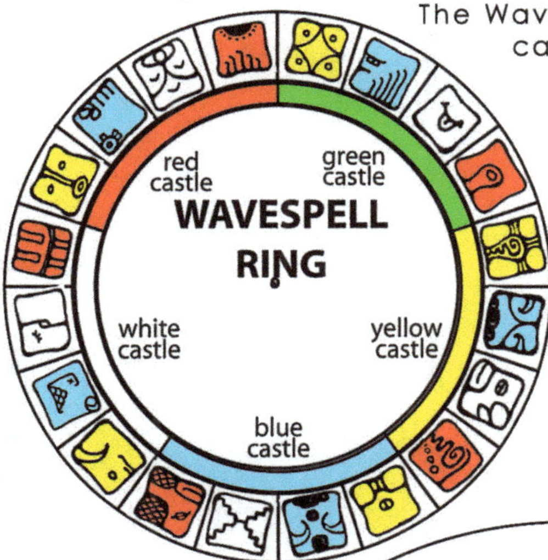

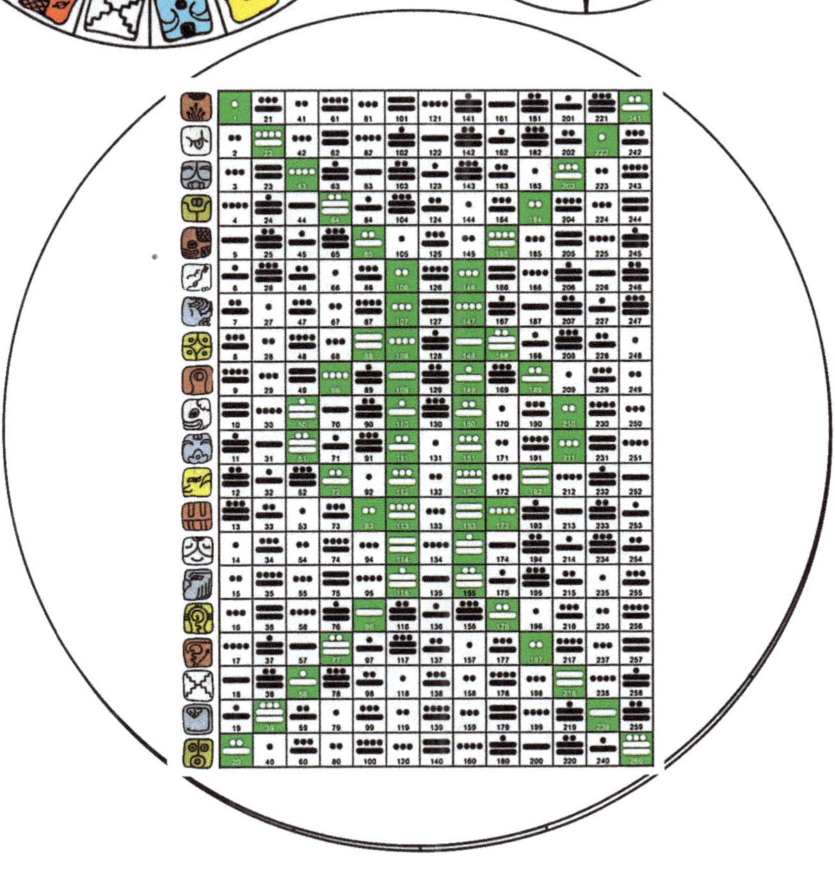

This book is dedicated to all
those who kept the codes alive,
to benefit the Earth now...

'Who owns your time
owns your mind;
own your own time
and know your own mind.'

—*Jose Arguelles/Valum Votan*

CPSIA information can be obtained
at www.ICGtesting.com
Printed in the USA
LVHW080811220221
679596LV00025B/1289